SPACE SHUTTLE

SCIENCE & TECHNOLOGY

BY WILBUR AND SUSANNA CROSS

CHILDRENS PRESS ™

CHICAGO

Space shuttle *Columbia*'s second launch, November 12, 1981

Library of Congress Cataloging in Publication Data

Cross, Wilbur and Susanna.
  Space shuttle.

  Includes index.
  Summary: Discusses the history and development of
the space shuttle, and how, by its "opening up" space,
every area of our lives will be affected.
  1. Astronautics—Juvenile literature. 2. Space
shuttles—Juvenile literature. [1. Space shuttles.
2. Astronautics] I. Cross, Susanna. II. Title.
TL793.C76 1985   629.44′1   84-7702
ISBN 0-516-00513-8

Editor: Ann Heinrichs Tomchek
Designer: Dolores Hollister

Picture Acknowledgements
All pictures courtesy of the National Aeronautics and
Space Administration (NASA), except the following:
Historical Pictures Service—23 right, 113 left
The Granger Collection—20, 23 left, 24
Susan Heinrichs—25
AP Photo from Moscow—27
AP Wirephoto—29, 73
Photo ESA—119

TABLE OF CONTENTS

INTRODUCTION

THE SPACE TRANSPORTATION SYSTEM

"With the first orbital flight of the Space Shuttle," wrote the former United States Senator Adlai E. Stevenson in 1979, "the curtain rises on an era that will shape U.S. space exploration for the next decade, and perhaps for the remainder of the century. . . . We will go into space not just to meet the challenge of exploration but to do many useful and productive jobs, at reduced cost, returning again and again."

Senator Stevenson, who was then the chairman of the Senate's Subcommittee on Science, Technology and Space, predicted that the space shuttle would be as different from earlier space vehicles as a modern ocean freighter is from Robert Fulton's first steamship, the *Clermont*.

Unlike its predecessors, *Mercury*, *Gemini*, and *Apollo*, the versatile space shuttle could be used over and over again. It could offer many useful years of service and thus bring space vehicles into the world of commercial transportation. The space shuttle can exploit space as a magnificent new resource, rather than a strange and hostile environment in which humans are overwhelmed.

One of the many advantages of putting space to use is the complete lack of gravity, a force that dominates human activity on earth. While gravity has many advantages, it also restricts us. It constrains our motion, separates fluids, and produces friction. The natural vacuum that exists in space—an almost total absence of matter—also has its

Left: Space shuttle *Columbia* ready for launch

advantages. These two factors make it possible to manufacture better materials, such as chemicals and drugs, in space. These materials, created under space conditions, are more pure and uniform than anything we can make on earth under the most ideal laboratory conditions.

Thus shuttle craft, with their ability to move quickly and effectively between earth and space, open up new benefits for all mankind. Raw materials carried into space will be brought back to earth with their chemical, thermal, optical, physical, and electrical properties more fully developed than ever before. This will help to achieve major breakthroughs in medicine, energy, electronics, instrumentation, and many other fields of science and construction.

When a special team from the National Aeronautics and Space Administration (NASA) reviewed the United States space program at the beginning of the 1980s, it named specific contributions that the space program could make in the next quarter of a century. These contributions, compiled in an official report, ranged from weather and communications to environmental protection, food production, energy and ore exploration, forestry management, enhancement of marine resources, and a better understanding of all the earth sciences.

Much of the progress foreseen in this report, *Outlook for Space*, hinged on the development of the Space Transportation System (NASA's name for the shuttle program and its many activities). One exciting concept was *Spacelab*, the manned space laboratory that will depend on shuttle craft for its very existence, as well as for transporting its products.

America started out slowly and overcautiously in the race to outer space. When the Soviets launched *Sputnik I*, the first man-made satellite, in 1957, America had little to show for its own efforts. Stunned by what the Russians had achieved so quickly and gloriously, the United States Congress created NASA to make up for lost time. By the time NASA had reached its twenty-fifth birthday in 1983, America had surpassed Russia and had become the acknowledged leader in space exploration. The scientific discoveries spearheaded by

NASA have created whole new industries and jobs, raised our standard of living, and improved our quality of life in many ways.

The Space Transportation System is shaping NASA's goals and programs in the last two decades of the twentieth century. In one sense, the space shuttle itself—so distinctive in design—is a realistic, and exciting, symbol of man's conquest of space.

"Man, that
was one
fantastic
ride!"

THE SPRINGBOARD

1

FIRST
FLIGHT

SHUTTLE LAUNCH CONTROL: Coming up on 10. T minus 10 . . . 9 . . . We are go for main engine start. We have main engine start. Minus 4 . . . 3 . . . 2 . . . 1. We have ignition. We have ignition of the solid rocket boosters and lift-off. Shuttle has cleared the tower. Mission Control now confirms all maneuvers started. Twenty seconds. Thrust looks good. Counting 25 seconds. Roll maneuver completed. Now 30 seconds. Columbia *one nautical mile in altitude.*

HOUSTON: Mark one minute, 55 seconds. Columbia *now 21 nautical miles in altitude, 18 nautical miles downrange. Velocity now reading 5,000 feet per second. Standing by now for solid rocket booster separation.*

COLUMBIA: It looks like we got a good solid rocket booster separation.

HOUSTON: Confirm. A good SRB separation.

COLUMBIA: Smooth as silk, Houston.

HOUSTON: Two minutes, 21 seconds. Onboard guidance is lining up as programmed. Columbia *is steering for its proper position in space for main engine cutoff.*

COLUMBIA: Sounds good. We're getting all pictures on the monitor.

HOUSTON: We read you loud and clear . . .

At 7:00 A.M., on April 12, 1981, the three main engines and two rocket boosters on the space shuttle generated 6.5 million pounds of upward thrust to lift *Columbia* from Launch Pad 39A at the Kennedy

Astronauts at the space shuttle flight deck

Space Center in Florida. Rising on a pillar of orange flame and white steam, the ship cleared its tall launch tower in just six seconds and was off on the first successful shuttle flight in history.

Some 12 minutes later, with the solid rocket boosters and the external fuel tank jettisoned, *Columbia* had reached orbit and was circling the earth.

"Man, that was one fantastic ride!" exclaimed the pilot, Robert L. Crippen, two-and-a-half days later. The space shuttle had just made a perfect landing on the hard-packed floor of a dry lake in California's Mojave Desert. But Crippen's excitement had already been recorded. During the blast-off, NASA's instruments in Houston showed that Crippen's heartbeat had increased from 60 to 130 beats per minute. The other crew member and commander, John W. Young, was excited too. But as a veteran of four previous flights, including an *Apollo* moon landing, Young was more accustomed to the thrill of the blast-off. His pulse rate only increased to 85.

LAUNCH OPERATIONS

After the space shuttle was positioned at the launch pad in Florida, it was carefully monitored from the nearby Launch Control Center. However, after the shuttle was launched and cleared the tower, the control was turned over to the Mission Control Center in Houston. Houston could monitor the shuttle no matter where it was around the globe.

It had been decided long before that this first flight, as well as the two to follow, would be for testing purposes only. *Columbia* would carry no "payload" in its wide cargo bay. Instead, it would carry instruments for measuring its performance while in orbit around the earth and during the final glide through the atmosphere to a landing. However, the clamshell-like doors on the 15- by 60-foot cargo bay would be tested in flight to make sure that they would open and latch properly under space conditions. The heat shield had to be tested, too. This shield would allow the ship to re-enter the earth's atmosphere without burning up.

As in all such ventures into outer space, there are three critical phases: (1) the launch itself, (2) orbiting the earth, and (3) the landing. A spacecraft not only has to adapt to the three different environments, but has to be able to move from one phase to the other without losing control or endangering the mission.

This first mission, known as STS-1, was unusual because it was the first time that an American spacecraft had gone into orbit without prior unmanned testing. For this reason, the whole mission was very carefully planned, with safety as the primary consideration. "The mission objectives," said NASA, "were a safe ascent and safe return of *Columbia* and its crew." Each step was painstakingly checked out in advance. NASA began assembling components for the launch, for example, a year and a half before the launch date.

The launch countdown itself was very detailed and thorough, starting fifteen hours before the lift-off. Some five hours ahead of time, the external fuel tank was carefully filled with highly volatile liquid

Columbia's cargo bay during door opening and closing exercises

oxygen and hydrogen. About two hours before the launch, everything was ready. The two-man crew was awakened from a preflight rest and boarded the *Columbia*. Not until about ten minutes ahead of the scheduled lift-off time, however, was the official order given: "Go for launch!" And even then, there were built-in alternatives so that the mission could be delayed at almost any time right down to the final few seconds.

Further safeguards included equipment for ejecting the two crew members so that they could parachute back to earth if serious flaws developed right after lift-off. There were also plans for the *Columbia* to glide back to earth before reaching orbit if the rocket systems failed.

MANEUVERING IN SPACE

Once in orbit, the space shuttle was easy to control by firing the Orbital Maneuvering System (OMS). This system could change the position and shape of the orbit. Young and Crippen used the OMS to change from the originally planned elliptical pattern to a circular orbit. They tested all the *Columbia*'s systems during some fifty-four hours in space and conducted numerous engineering tests. They checked the computers and the jet thrusters, which were used to turn the shuttle from one position to another as it circled the globe. For the most part, *Columbia* was flown upside-down in relation to the earth. This way, Young and Crippen had a better view of the earth and its horizon and could navigate the ship properly.

Young and Crippen documented their flight with still pictures and films, which provided valuable information on the shuttle's performance. One sequence showed, for example, that sixteen of the heat-shielding tiles on the outside of the shuttle had been loosened and lost during the stress of the launch. These tiles are critical in protecting the craft when it re-enters the earth's atmosphere. On re-entry, the shuttle is subjected to friction and heat as intense as 3,000 degrees Fahrenheit. The tiles are made of a material that sheds heat so efficiently that they can be red-hot on one side, yet cool enough on the other side to be touched with the bare hand.

Columbia's first on-board photo, looking back across the cargo bay. The left and right Orbital Maneuvering System (OMS) pods appear on either side of the tail fin. This photo revealed that several heat-shielding tiles were missing from the OMS pods.

TRACKING THE FLIGHT

How could Mission Control in Houston, Texas, monitor a flight that for the most part was orbiting other parts of the globe? The answer is STDN—Spaceflight Tracking and Data Network. This is a highly complex worldwide system that provided continuous, instantaneous, and completely reliable communications with the space shuttle and its crew. This network was maintained and operated by NASA's Goddard Space Flight Center in Greenbelt, Maryland. It consisted of eighteen ground stations, some in the United States and some in other countries, including Australia, Bermuda, Botswana, Chile, Ecuador, Senegal, Spain, and the United Kingdom.

The Network Operations Control Center at the Goddard base could also serve as an emergency mission control center, in case Mission Control in Houston was impaired for any reason. Besides the network of tracking stations, there were other stations throughout the world that assisted with specific maneuvers. The stations in Spain, the Indian Ocean, Australia, and Guam, for example, provided special information and support for the orbital maneuvering—the pattern of orbiting around the earth. Other stations, in California and along the West Coast, assisted in the shuttle's re-entry into the earth's atmosphere and its eventual landing in the desert.

Goddard Space Flight Center also operated the NASA Communications Network (NASCOM). This consisted of more than two million miles of communications channels. It included domestic and foreign communications satellites, submarine cables, long land lines, and microwave radio systems. These channels connected all the tracking stations, launch and orbital control centers, and other supporting locations. The main switching center at Goddard directed the entire communications network with the support of NASCOM switching centers in Madrid, Spain; Canberra, Australia; the Jet Propulsion Laboratory at Pasadena, California; and the Air Force communications centers at Cape Canaveral, Florida, and Vandenberg Air Force Base, California.

Computers at all the supporting stations were constantly "talking" to each other and to the spacecraft at split-second intervals. They relayed all instrument readings so that everyone in the communications network could observe the progress of *Columbia*, orbiting at a relatively low altitude of about 150 miles above the earth. At Mission Control Center, computers could detect even the slightest change in instrument readings. These readings were instantly compared with stored information programs to show how much they differed from the planned functions. The computers also provided visual, on-screen displays for the mission personnel to view.

Television cameras aboard the space shuttle fed live images to the tracking stations below. They showed a variety of activities, such as the cargo bay door being opened, closed, and latched, the forward flight deck with the two astronauts at their controls, Crippen preparing a meal on the mid deck, and a view of the earth through the cockpit window as Young operated the jet thrusters to change the angle of the craft.

"We could see almost everything about the flight and the performance of *Columbia*," said one ground controller, "just as if we had been floating alongside the ship in space and watching what was going on. In a way, it was kind of eerie."

RETURN TO EARTH

Shortly after noon on April 14, Young and Crippen fired the craft's orbital maneuvering rockets for two and a half minutes to reduce their speed from 17,500 miles per hour. They were over the Indian Ocean and ready to begin their hour-long descent to the landing area on Rogers Dry Lake in California's Mojave Desert.

Then they fired the jet thrusters to turn *Columbia* from its upside-down position, so that it was right-side up and ready to approach the landing strip in much the same way that a plane does. There was one significant difference, however. As the shuttle started to enter the earth's atmosphere, it reached what is known as the "entry interface," at an altitude of some 400,000 feet. This is the crucial point where earth's gravity takes hold and the enveloping air causes immense friction. At this moment, Young and Crippen fired the jet thrusters again in order to pitch the craft's nose upward 40 degrees. In this position, the well-protected underside of the ship would bear the brunt of the atmospheric pressures and extremely high temperatures caused by increasing friction. All this work took place over the western Pacific Ocean, while the shuttle was still far from the landing strip.

After the fiery entry into the earth's atmosphere, the ship's computers automatically triggered a major change in the control system. The jet thrusters and the orbital maneuvering rockets were shut down.

The end of *Columbia*'s first flight: orbiter landing on Rogers Dry Lake in the Mojave Desert (left); pilot Robert Crippen approaching the medical van (right).

In their place, the computers activated the ship's rudder and elevons. (Elevons are a combination of the ailerons and elevators that control an aircraft's flight.) The ninety-eight-ton *Columbia* then began to function like an enormous glider. Air drag caused it to lose speed steadily as it approached the landing strip.

According to a carefully rehearsed plan, the pilots guided the craft over Rogers Dry Lake, then banked sharply to the left and looped back. This maneuver put the space shuttle in the right position for landing. It would touch down at about 215 miles per hour, or twice the landing speed of a commercial jetliner. This was the first airplane-like landing of any craft from an orbit in space.

The historic flight had taken two days, six hours, twenty minutes, and fifty-two seconds from the time of the lift-off at Cape Canaveral, Florida.

But the flight was not quite over. As soon as *Columbia* stopped rolling along the hard-packed lake bed, it was surrounded by a convoy of vehicles carrying a variety of specialists. Their first job was to ventilate the cargo bay and spaces surrounding the engines. This was to remove any accumulated gases that might be explosive or poisonous. They then carefully removed all leftover fuel from the engines in order to prevent accidental fires. It took about an hour to make sure that no hazards remained. Only then was the side hatch opened and the crew permitted to leave the craft. They were ushered to a waiting medical van and taken to a clinic for complete physical examinations. It was vital to know whether their experience in space had affected their bodies in any way.

One of the greatest concerns, for both the ground crew and the shuttle crew, had been whether the heat-shielding tiles on the nose and underside of the shuttle would absorb the sudden rise in temperature during re-entry. As it turned out, the tiles withstood temperatures as high as 3,000 degrees Fahrenheit without cracking or flaking. After inspecting *Columbia*, NASA technicians reported that it was in excellent condition. And they found no reason why the shuttle could not make one hundred more round trips between earth and earth orbit.

This was good news. One of the objectives of the Space Shuttle program is to save money by using the same equipment over and over. This places the shuttle in the same category as a plane, ready to make scheduled runs on a regular basis. Even the two solid rocket boosters that were used during takeoff and jettisoned before reaching orbit were recovered for future flights. Equipped with parachutes, the boosters floated gently down to the ocean and were picked up in the Atlantic, off Daytona Beach, Florida.

On November 12, 1981, *Columbia* became the first space vehicle in history to be used more than once. Although this second flight was shortened because of a fuel cell problem, most of the mission's goals were achieved. One goal was to test a huge mechanical arm installed over the cargo bay and operated by controls in the flight deck. The arm was designed to lift equipment from the storage bay and put it into orbit, or to retrieve items in orbit that were to be brought back to earth. The arm was also designed to reach around and inspect the exterior of the shuttle.

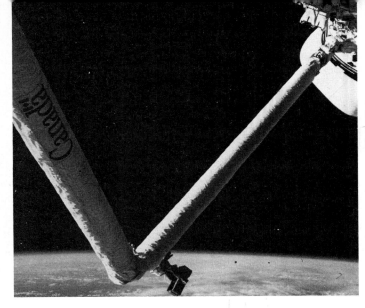

First workout of the Canadian-made remote manipulator system (RMS) arm. The arm was equipped with its own lighting system and closed-circuit television (see camera near "elbow"), so the crew could closely observe its operation.

The mechanical arm was jointed, just the way a human arm is jointed at the shoulder, elbow, and wrist. About fifteen inches in diameter, it could be stretched fifty feet when fully extended, and weighed some nine hundred pounds. Its "hand," called an "end effector," consisted mainly of a wire device that could be tightened around hooks on the items in the cargo bay. The robot arm was tested both manually and using a computer that was programmed for a planned series of movements.

Besides conducting engineering tests, the crew of the second *Columbia* flight made important earth surveys. They experimented in such fields as exploring for oil and gas, prospecting for minerals, locating better ocean fishing grounds, forecasting the weather, and measuring air pollution. These experiments proved that the space shuttle was a stable and reliable "platform" in space for conducting many kinds of earth surveys.

One important improvement in the second flight of *Columbia* involved the heat-shielding tiles that protected the craft during re-entry. The nearly 31,000 tiles were redesigned and cemented before the flight. During the flight, none of these tiles was lost and only a dozen were damaged enough to need replacement.

It was more evident than ever that the nation's new Space Transportation System was off to a good start.

BEFORE THE SHUTTLE

2
A HISTORY OF SPACE EXPLORATION

During the battle of Kaifeng, in northern China, Mongol hordes were fiercely attacking the Chinese defenders. Suddenly, their charge was disrupted when they found themselves attacked by a terrifying deluge of ''fire arrows.'' The year was 1230 and these new, unheard-of weapons of war were what today are called skyrockets—long sticks propelled through the air by burning gunpowder.

This was possibly the first effective use of rockets in history. Word of this devastating new invention spread throughout Asia. The Chinese were credited with having developed black powder explosive enough to thrust the arrows against oncoming enemy troops. The first use of rockets in Europe is said to have been in the year 1241 during a Tatar attack against Poles in the battle of Liegnitz. Accounts are vague, but we do know that rockets were known all over Europe by the end of the thirteenth century. Often called ''flying fire'' or ''wildfire,'' their major purpose was to set fire to enemy encampments or to the wooden buildings in a city.

The word ''rocket'' was first used in Italy, where the ''flying fire'' was highly effective during the Venetian-Genovese war in 1379. It was called *rocchetta*, meaning a ''small staff,'' and referring to the fiery stick that was propelled through the air. After the middle of the fifteenth century, the rocket seems to have fallen into disuse as a weapon. But it was being put to other uses, mainly for fireworks displays.

Left: From a 19ᵗʰ-century edition of Jules Verne's *From the Earth to the Moon*

During this time, people began thinking of the rocket as a possible device to assist in one of man's oldest dreams, to fly through the air like a bird. Although it is probably pure fiction, the legend of Wan Hu illustrates this trend of thought. Wan Hu was a wealthy Chinese landowner with many servants. He invented a chairlike device attached to two kites and containing forty-three rockets around its base. Seating himself on this unlikely contraption, with the kites flying high above him, he had forty-three of his servants light the rockets simultaneously.

They did as instructed. There was a frightening explosion, followed by clouds of smoke. By the time the smoke had cleared away, Wan Hu had vanished, along with chair, kites, and rockets. He was never seen again.

Legend has it that he rocketed to the land of gods, which is probably about as close to the truth as could be.

THE CONCEPT OF ROCKETS AND SPACE FLIGHT

In 1678, the famed British mathematician Sir Isaac Newton published *Principia*, a monumental discussion of science and technology that is considered a classic. His explanation of the principle of rocket propulsion provided the first scientific basis for the development of rockets. He even described how a projectile, if propelled far enough above the earth, would go into orbit and not be pulled back down by gravity.

Newton was far ahead of his time, and it was not until two centuries later that dreams of space flight really began to capture the public imagination. Oddly enough, they were stimulated not by a scientist, but by one of the most popular writers of the day, Jules Verne. Two of his books, *From the Earth to the Moon*, published in 1865, and its sequel, *Round the Moon*, published five years later, captivated readers with the idea that space flight was within the realm of achievement, perhaps in their own lifetime.

Robert H. Goddard (on stepladder), directing adjustments on one of his rockets near Roswell, New Mexico. *Right:* Goddard and his first liquid-fuel rocket.

It is interesting that Verne's version of the spaceship was named *Columbiad*, and that the three-man crew experienced weightlessness while in orbit and before making a safe landing in the ocean.

The next important step did not occur until after the turn of the century, when the Russians, French, Germans, Belgians, and Americans all attempted to design aircraft that could successfully utilize the rocket principle. In 1912, an American physicist, Robert H. Goddard, began his rocket experiments. Within two years, he had made two important contributions. The first was a patent for a liquid-fuel rocket. The second was a design for a rocket with two or more stages. His idea was that the firing of these stages would propel the rocket farther than any single charge, no matter how large it might be.

Goddard's first treatise, "A Method for Reaching Extreme Altitudes," was published by the Smithsonian Institution in 1920. In March, 1926, Goddard successfully fired the first liquid-fuel rocket, a feat that was not equalled by any other inventors until five years later.

Robert H. Goddard (at left) checking the fuel pumps of a rocket at his Roswell, New Mexico, research center.

Another pioneer was Konstantin E. Tsiolkovsky of Russia, who not only described the technology of practical space flight, but was a convincing writer of science-fiction stories, based on his scientific studies. His classic, *Beyond the Earth*, published in 1916, accurately described the kind of interplanetary travel that was not to take place for four decades. His descriptions included ways to minimize the impact of the launch, methods for controlling spaceships in orbit, and the use of retrofire rockets to slow the craft on re-entry into the earth's atmosphere.

Tsiolkovsky's work, though little known outside of his own country, did much to motivate the Soviet Union. In 1929 they created the first government laboratory for the study of astronautics. Ironically, that same year, Dr. Goddard was receiving disrespectful mention in the press as the "moon rocket man" and was prohibited by the Massachusetts fire marshal from firing any more rockets in that state.

Fortunately for America, the noted Guggenheim family became deeply interested in Goddard's work and provided financial support. Goddard moved to a ranch near Roswell, New Mexico, where he successfully continued a great deal of vital research until 1941. The Guggenheims also helped to establish pioneering rocket development at the California Institute of Technology under another pioneer, Theodore von Karman.

Rockets, as applied to space travel, are divided into three categories. A rocket that can reach a maximum velocity of two miles per second is capable of rising into the upper atmosphere. If one or more stages are added so that the rocket can attain a velocity of five miles per second, it becomes a satellite vehicle. That is, it can go into orbit around the earth. If a rocket's speed is further increased to seven miles per second, then it is capable of going to the moon or into orbit around the sun or a distant planet. The space shuttle fits into the second category—a satellite vehicle, not capable of going beyond the earth's orbit.

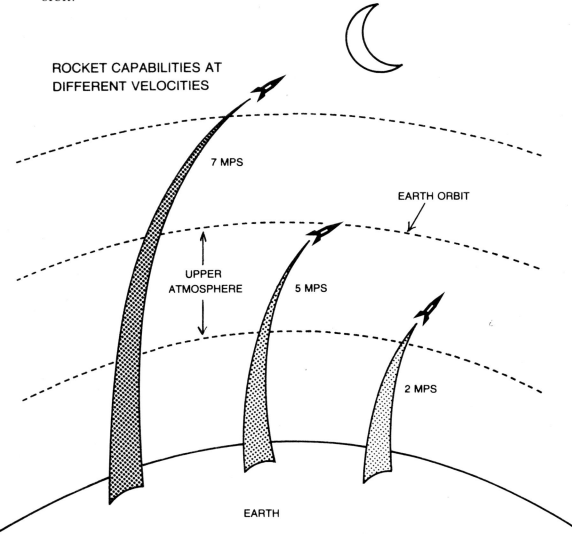

ROCKET CAPABILITIES AT
DIFFERENT VELOCITIES

7 MPS

EARTH ORBIT

UPPER
ATMOSPHERE

5 MPS

2 MPS

EARTH

BIRTH OF THE SPACE AGE

If the Space Age has a birthday, it is October 4, 1957. On that day, Russia launched the first man-made satellite, *Sputnik I* (meaning "fellow traveler"). By present-day standards, it was a very simple spacecraft, a sphere only twenty-two inches in diameter. Made of aluminum alloys, it weighed a mere 184 pounds and contained two radio transmitters and chemical batteries. It was launched by a military rocket that had been adapted for this special purpose. Once it was in orbit, it varied from about 158 miles to 142 miles above the earth.

The event was startling in a number of significant ways. First, it demonstrated that the most obstinate barrier of all had been broken and that humans *could* send a vehicle into orbit. Second, it came as a complete surprise to the American public, and even to most officials of the United States government, including those who were working in this field. The United States knew that the Russians were trying to launch a man-made satellite, but most experts did not think that a successful launch would take place soon.

When *Sputnik I* was launched, there was not a single radio-tracking system in the U.S. on a frequency that could follow the satellite in orbit. In the words of one critic, "The United States was caught with its antennas down."

The Russian achievement was headlined on the front page of just about every daily newspaper in the world. "*Sputnik I*," said a paper published later by the Smithsonian Institution, "was certainly the most widely publicized achievement of modern science."

The Russians made history again, one month later, with the launching of *Sputnik II*. Not only was this satellite much larger—more than one thousand pounds—but it transported the first living being into space, a dog named Laika. Laika's condition while in orbit was transmitted to earth in detail, for the dog was monitored by scientific instruments that gave readings on its heartbeat, blood pressure, and respiration.

Laika, ready for a space trip in *Sputnik II*

Public reaction to *Sputnik I* was described by the Smithsonian Astrophysical Observatory in Cambridge, Massachusetts, as "a strange mixture of awe, admiration, and fear, the last enhanced, of course, because there had been no warning." The observatory received thousands of letters and hundreds of phone calls about *Sputnik*. Many people had trouble believing that the Russians, whom they considered backward and still trying to recover from the devastation of World War II, had the technical capability to launch an artificial satellite. After all, the United States had not yet achieved this and, in fact, still seemed far away from any promising attempt.

"Others were openly fearful," said the Smithsonian. "They believed that *Sputnik I* carried either atom bombs to destroy the United States or television cameras to spy on her. Not a few felt that the scientist was once again meddling in cosmic affairs that were not his business."

What this reaction showed, more than anything else, was that people were not yet used to the idea of space conquest—even though science fiction was highly popular and voyages to outer space appeared regularly in books, in movies, and on TV. If the United States had been first in space, the public would have had plenty of warning. They would have been ready for such an event, and would have followed every step of the launch and orbit. As it was, not knowing about *Sputnik* in advance and worrying about the Soviets' intentions gave the American public a negative outlook on what was a truly historic event.

As America recovered from the shock of the *Sputnik* launch, the public was reassured to hear that the U.S. had an answer to *Sputnik*—Project Vanguard, which was ready to launch a satellite from Cape Canaveral, Florida. The promise was confirmed when, at 10:30 in the morning of December 6, 1957, the rocket (actually "Vanguard Test Vehicle #3") stood on the launching pad, only one hour away from firing.

The monstrous gantry crane, weighing hundreds of tons, was slowly moved back, leaving the rocket in full view. The countdown began: T minus 60 minutes . . . T minus 50 . . . T minus 40 . . . T minus 10.

With five minutes to go, ice began forming on the rocket near the liquid-oxygen tank (a normal action), covering it with a frosty coat. The controllers were tense, but beginning to show relief that everything was proceeding well. Then, with less than sixty seconds to go, the needle of the wind recorder kicked up suddenly. Unexpected gusts of wind were swirling across the launch area.

"HOLD!" The order rang out and the countdown stopped temporarily. All eyes were on the wind gauge.

The countdown finally began again. T minus 45 seconds . . . T minus 30 . . . T minus 20. At T minus 1 the order was given: "FIRE!" This time the rocket engine showed sparks and fire. This was accompanied by a heart-rending, whining moan, like some great beast in pain. Flame built up, red, then brilliantly white. The space vehicle shook and howled and began to rise.

"Look out! Oh, no!" shouted one of the controllers.

Red flames shot out from the side of the rocket, near the engine. The giant vehicle quivered and heaved, then began to sink like a great sword down into the blast tube. It broke apart with a gigantic roar. The ground trembled and a shock wave rattled the thick glass protecting the observers in the control station. Within seconds, *Vanguard* was a pile of smoldering scrap metal.

Vanguard rocket going up in flames on Dec. 6, 1957. Less than 10 seconds elapsed between the first picture, taken before firing, and the last picture, showing the smoke cloud drifting into the sky.

Americans would not get over their dismay at this catastrophe until January 31, 1958. On that date, the United States finally succeeded in launching the first American satellite, *Explorer 1*, into orbit. This was followed by the successful launching of a *Vanguard* space vehicle on March 17, 1958, and a second satellite nine days later.

The biggest American milestone that year was the birth of the National Aeronautics and Space Administration. NASA was to be the guiding light and motivating force behind America's many achievements in space from the end of the 1950s to the present day. These successes were to include unmanned space probes that discovered phenomena such as radiation belts and magnetic fields in outer space and transmitted the information back to earth; unmanned landings on the moon to transmit televised pictures of the lunar surface; and ultimately the historic landing of astronauts on the moon.

Scientist-astronaut Owen K. Garriott during extravehicular activity on *Skylab 3*

In 1961, President John F. Kennedy initiated the Apollo moon program, the largest scientific undertaking in American history. Its goal was dramatically fulfilled on July 20, 1969, when two astronauts, Neil A. Armstrong and Edwin E. Aldrin, Jr., stepped out onto the surface of the moon. In all, there were seventeen Apollo missions. Some were unmanned experiments to test equipment and operations and others were lunar landings. Because of the constant television coverage, people all over the world were able to see just what it was like to venture into outer space and walk on the moon.

SKYLAB

After the Apollo Program was completed, the United States continued manned space exploration with *Skylab*. This was an orbiting space station that served as a workshop with living quarters for three astronauts. Initially, the main capsule was launched into space unmanned. Later, in May, 1973, the first astronauts arrived in an *Apollo*-type vehicle, which they docked alongside *Skylab*. The three-man crews remained in the capsule for periods of one, two, or three months over a nine-month period (the useful life of *Skylab 1*).

Skylab 3 over Brazil's Amazon River Valley (*right*)

The *Skylab* crews conducted numerous experiments, and used solar telescopes to study the earth, solar flares, and natural resources. But their overall objective was to study and evaluate the ability of humans to live for long periods in space and cope with prolonged conditions of weightlessness.

BIRTH OF THE SPACE SHUTTLE

In September, 1969, a few months after the first manned lunar landing, President Richard Nixon appointed a Space Task Group to study the country's future course in space research and exploration. The Task Group recommended that "the United States should . . . develop new systems of technology for space operation . . . through a program directed initially towards development of a new space transportation capability."

A few months later, NASA made extensive studies of a new kind of space vehicle, which was to be called the "space shuttle." The studies covered a wide range of possible designs and sizes, and gradually focused on the now-familiar delta-wing design—a spacecraft that looked more like a jetliner or a military jet than the space capsules of the past.

In January, 1972, the president announced that NASA would build a shuttle system that would be both reusable and low in cost—largely because the shuttle could make round trips again and again with very little modification or repair. The space shuttle would use two solid-propellant rocket motors, which operated at a lower cost and risk than other types.

The first shuttle, known as an "orbiter" because most of its life would be spent in orbit around the earth, was named *Enterprise*. Completed in September, 1976, it was designed as a test and demonstration model, to prove that the craft could both fly in orbit and land as a glider. It was not, however, designed for launch into space. *Enterprise* went through three demonstration stages:

(1) Five "captive" flights in which it was mounted, unmanned, atop a large aircraft, known as a "carrier." Each flight tested such factors as wind resistance, wing lift, and airflow design.

(2) Three similar flights, but with two-man crews operating and checking all of the control systems.

(3) Five free flights, in which *Enterprise*, with crews aboard, was released from the carrier and maneuvered to a glider landing.

Test flight of the orbiter *Enterprise*, riding piggyback on a jet

This prototype of the space shuttle was subjected to hundreds of tests. It was vibrated to determine how well it held together under stress. It was joined to an external tank and solid rocket boosters to make certain that these components were properly designed. It was boarded by crews who checked out the arrangement of instruments and equipment.

NASA announced that the first space shuttles would be named after sailing ships. In order of appearance, they would be:

Columbia, named after a Navy frigate launched in 1836 and one of the first American sailing ships to sail around the world.

Challenger, named after a Navy vessel that explored the Atlantic and Pacific oceans from 1872 to 1876.

Discovery, named after two ships: Henry Hudson's, which in 1610 searched for a Northwest Passage between the Atlantic and Pacific oceans; and Captain James Cook's, which discovered the Hawaiian Islands and explored southern Alaska and western Canada.

Atlantis, named after a two-masted ketch operated by the Woods Hole Oceanographic Institute from 1930 until 1966.

With this kind of history behind them, the space shuttles had a remarkable heritage to live up to. So far, they are already accomplishing this high-level goal admirably.

THE MAGNIFICENT MACHINE

3

"After more than 900,000 miles, the body was a little scorched and needed some cosmetic repairs, and the plumbing did not work quite right," said an article in the October, 1981, issue of *Discover* magazine, "but the space shuttle *Columbia* still looked like a bargain to astronaut Richard Truly."

Truly, who with Joe Engle was to make up the crew of the second shuttle mission into space, said of *Columbia* after the ship's historic first mission, "I wish I could buy a used car that looks as good as this does."

These comments, in a nutshell, point to one of the major objectives of NASA's shuttle program: to develop a fleet of space vehicles that will be used for many missions, yet require minimum repair and maintenance between flights. When you consider it, the goal is no less than astronomical: a space shuttle, designed to undertake a minimum of one hundred missions, will eventually clock some 90 million miles before it is taken out of service!

The versatile space shuttle is a true aerospace vehicle. It is launched like a rocket; it maneuvers in earth's orbit like a spacecraft; and it lands like a glider. No such machine has ever existed before, or even been conceived of until very recently. Besides having capabilities for research and exploration, it has one great advantage over previous space vehicles: it can carry heavy loads into orbit and bring back other loads—just like the major forms of transportation on earth. Other space vehicles have done this, but they were not designed for repeat performances at increasingly lower costs.

Left: Launch of the ninth shuttle mission on November 28, 1983

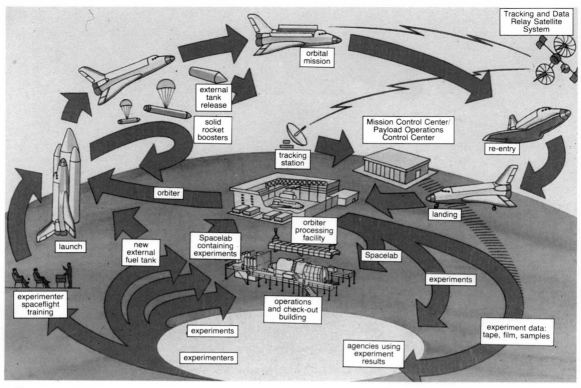

Tracking and Data
Relay Satellite
System

orbital
mission

external
tank
release

solid
rocket
boosters

Mission Control Center/
Payload Operations
Control Center

re-entry

tracking
station

orbiter

landing

launch

new
external
fuel tank

Spacelab
containing
experiments

orbiter
processing
facility

Spacelab

experiments

experimenter
spaceflight
training

operations
and check-out
building

experiments

experiment data:
tape, film, samples

experimenters

agencies using
experiment
results

There are many support operations behind every shuttle mission.

The space shuttle can check out and fix unmanned satellites in orbit, or else bring them back to earth for repair. This alone will save millions of dollars, since costly and highly complicated satellites can be repaired instead of replaced. Shuttles can rendezvous with and maintain many types of vehicles. These include satellites working on environmental protection, energy exploration, weather forecasting, navigation, oceanography, mapping the earth, and many other vital operations. Shuttles will save millions of dollars by making this kind of research more effective.

Interplanetary spacecraft can be placed in earth orbit by the shuttles, together with a rocket stage. After all systems are checked out and the craft is in proper orbit, the rocket is fired, accelerating the interplanetary craft into deep space. This rocket, called the Inertial Upper Stage (IUS), can also be used to boost satellites to higher orbits than the maximum altitude of the shuttles, which is six hundred miles above the earth.

Each shuttle has a short turnaround time. That is, it can make a trip into orbit, return to earth, and be ready to go into space again within a few weeks. Eventually this turnaround time may take just a few days—almost like a jetliner with its regular flight schedules and maintenance periods. This flexibility is important. It will allow scientists to observe important, but fleeting, astronomical events or to study drastic weather changes, floods, unexplained air pollution, or other environmental crises on earth. Using the information collected on the shuttle, scientists can evaluate the problems and find solutions much more quickly and effectively than ever before.

Space shuttles also bring within scientists' practical grasp projects that were little more than dreams a few years ago. They can, for example, transport into orbit all the components needed to construct large solar power stations to convert the sun's energy into electricity. This would greatly reduce the constant demand for petroleum and coal. Think of this kind of operation as similar to the construction of a prefabricated house. The parts are all manufactured individually at one location, then brought to the building site some distance away for assembly. In the case of a solar power station in space, the same method is followed. The technical and mechanical components are assembled on earth by specialists. The parts are then carried by the space shuttle to an orbiting position around the earth. Another space shuttle brings a crew of technicians to the site, where they fit all the pieces in place.

In some cases, space shuttles might transport the components for small housing settlements. These would consist of modular housing units where workers and technicians could live temporarily while constructing solar power stations or other structures in space.

These are only a few of the endless possibilities.

SPACE SHUTTLE COMPONENTS

The magnificent machine known as the space shuttle is in one way very complex, since it is composed of so many different elements and back-up systems. Yet in another way, it is really a simple, compact vehicle. It has three main units: (1) the orbiter, or the airplane-like body with its giant tail, delta-shaped wings, and three main engines; (2) the external tank, which feeds propellants (liquid hydrogen and oxygen) to the engines during the first stage of flight; and (3) two solid rocket boosters that provide the energy for the initial lift-off.

The orbiter, which is about 120 feet long, with a wingspan of 80 feet, is roughly the size of a DC-9 commercial jetliner. It weighs approximately 150,000 pounds without fuel, and can carry a payload of 65,000 pounds in its cargo bay.

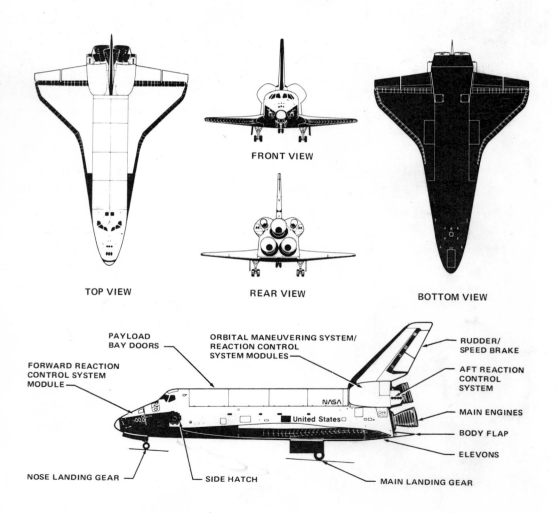

FRONT VIEW

TOP VIEW   REAR VIEW   BOTTOM VIEW

PAYLOAD BAY DOORS

ORBITAL MANEUVERING SYSTEM/ REACTION CONTROL SYSTEM MODULES

RUDDER/ SPEED BRAKE

FORWARD REACTION CONTROL SYSTEM MODULE

AFT REACTION CONTROL SYSTEM

MAIN ENGINES

BODY FLAP

ELEVONS

NOSE LANDING GEAR

SIDE HATCH

MAIN LANDING GEAR

Shuttle orbiter jettisoning its external fuel tank. The tank eventually falls into a remote area of the ocean.

The external tank is about 155 feet long and 29 feet in diameter. At the time of launching, it contains more than 1.5 million pounds of hydrogen and oxygen, each in separate compartments. During lift-off, the shuttle rides piggyback on the tank, which is jettisoned (dropped off) about ten minutes off the launch pad after its fuel has been consumed. The tank is the only part of the shuttle system that is not recovered and reused.

The two solid rocket boosters, which are about 165 feet long, are positioned alongside the tank. They operate in parallel with the main engines for the first two minutes of flight to provide the additional thrust needed for the orbiter to escape the gravitational pull of the earth. At an altitude of about twenty-four nautical miles, the two boosters separate from the orbiter and the external tank and descend to the ocean on parachutes. They are recovered by a waiting vessel and restored to use again.

The heart of the booster is the solid rocket motor, the largest of its type ever built for space flight. Together, the two motors can develop

A segment of the first solid rocket booster (left), ready for assembly at Kennedy Space Center. The solid rocket boosters (right) separate from the shuttle at an altitude of 24 nautical miles and parachute into the ocean.

a thrust of almost 5.5 million pounds at lift-off and sustain it until the shuttle is well on its way toward orbit. The propellant used is actually a solid, not a liquid, and is considered very safe. Known as PBAN, the propellant looks and feels much like a hard rubber eraser and is, in fact, partly made of synthetic rubber.

THE PARACHUTE RECOVERY SYSTEM

One of the interesting features of the solid rocket booster is the nose cap, which contains three separate parachute systems: a pilot parachute, a drogue parachute, and three main parachutes. The parachutes are unusual in design, made of concentric circles of nylon ribbon, spaced like venetian blinds. This ribbon construction provides the great strength needed for operation at high speeds.

When the rocket booster has reached a certain altitude, a barometric switch releases the nose cap. The pilot parachute opens into its small canopy, about 12 feet in diameter. Then the drogue parachute opens, with a diameter of about 54 feet. Next, the barometric switch opens the compartment containing the three main parachutes, each of which has a diameter of 115 feet. The boosters initially descend at almost 240 miles per hour. Then, the parachutes slow the descent to about 70 miles per hour. Finally atmospheric pressure slows the boosters down to 60 miles per hour as they approach sea level.

STRUCTURE OF THE ORBITER

The space shuttle itself is divided into three major sections: (1) the forward fuselage, containing the crew cabin and operational instruments; (2) the mid fuselage with its huge cargo bay, robot arm, and delta wing; and (3) the aft fuselage, with its tall vertical stabilizer, the three main engines, the maneuvering jet thrusters, and the wing's control sections. Most of the orbiter's parts are made of conventional aluminum, similar to that used in military and commercial jets.

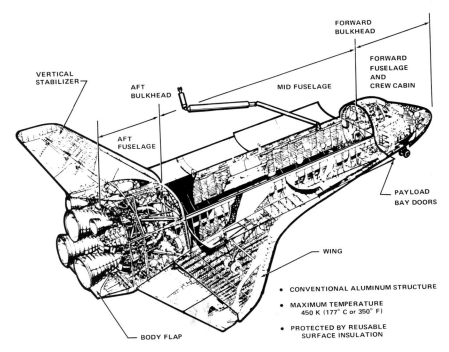

FORWARD BULKHEAD

FORWARD FUSELAGE AND CREW CABIN

VERTICAL STABILIZER

AFT BULKHEAD

MID FUSELAGE

AFT FUSELAGE

PAYLOAD BAY DOORS

WING

BODY FLAP

- CONVENTIONAL ALUMINUM STRUCTURE
- MAXIMUM TEMPERATURE 450 K (177° C or 350° F)
- PROTECTED BY REUSABLE SURFACE INSULATION

A typical space shuttle has a total length of about 120 feet, a height of 57 feet, and a wingspan of 80 feet. This is a rather modest size, considering the enormity of the projects that can be completed in orbit during a conventional flight.

FORWARD FUSELAGE

The forward fuselage is a pressurized area, much like the forward compartment of a jetliner. It contains the crew's living quarters, a laboratory area for conducting experiments, and the flight deck where the crew operates all the instruments that control the shuttle.

Either the pilot or the copilot can control the shuttle from their seats in the flight deck. In an emergency, a single crew member can fly the craft. Normally, the flight deck seats four people comfortably. There are more than two thousand separate controls and displays in the flight deck—over three times the number required for the Apollo command module on a trip to the moon! These include switches, circuit breakers, pushbuttons, thumb wheels, indicator lights, and meters.

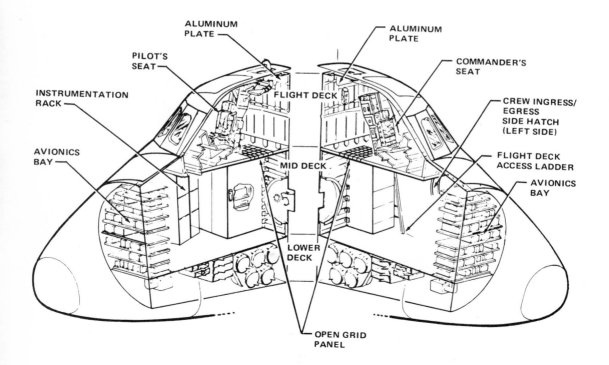

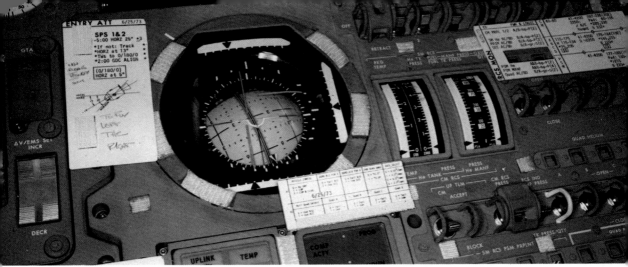

The shuttle flight deck has more than 2,000 controls and displays.

From the flight deck, the crew can open and close the bay doors, manipulate the robot arm, place objects in orbit from the bay, or grasp and store objects that are to be brought back to earth. Closed-circuit television screens provide live pictures of all the actions taking place and the positions of equipment and cargo. Visual control is especially critical when the space shuttle is retrieving instruments or modules from space and stowing them aboard.

Directly under the flight deck is the mid deck. It contains sleeping stations for the crew, storage compartments for provisions, a disposal system for getting rid of wastes, a personal hygiene station, and a table that can be used either for dining or for working. Although the normal crew size is seven people, at least three additional people can be seated in the combined crew and flight decks in an emergency.

The crew can move between flight deck and mid deck through two hatches. They must go through an air lock, however, to reach the payload bay, which is not pressurized. Air locks can be installed for activities outside the space shuttle. The air locks are roomy enough so that two crew members at a time can change into space suits there before leaving the craft. A special transfer tunnel can also be installed, so that the crew can move freely between the pressurized forward cabin and, say, a *Spacelab* with which the space shuttle has docked.

Astronaut C. Gordon Fullerton in the zero-gravity environment of the mid-deck, putting on a special suit for re-entry.

AVIONICS

Stored throughout each space shuttle, but largely in the forward fuselage, are the brains of this remarkable machine, technically known as the avionics system. The astronauts refer to these electrical and electronic devices as the "black boxes." Half a dozen of them are computers that are constantly "talking" to each other and keeping tabs on the shuttle and its equipment. Others are navigational instruments that guide the craft in its flight. Still others track stars, monitor the power units, handle communications with controllers on earth, store information, or compile environmental data.

The "black boxes" act as invisible members of the crew, controlling just about every system on board. They can automatically control flight during every phase of a mission except docking. The crew always has the option, though, of flying the shuttle manually.

A crucial factor in the design of these "black boxes" is their ability to withstand shock and breakdowns. They are designed with "redundant hardware," which means that when a component starts to fail it is automatically replaced by a back-up unit. It is as though a car had duplicate parts so that if a tire had a blowout, it would be immediately replaced with no interruption in driving.

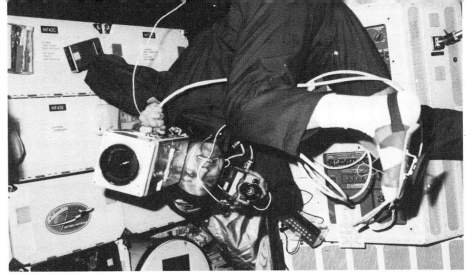

Astronaut Thomas K. Mattingly II holding a TV camera (left) and a 16mm camera. Note the suction-cup footwear.

More than two hundred of these electronic "black boxes" are connected to the computers through common party lines called "data buses." The status of individual components is constantly checked by one computer program. If there is any deviation from normal operation, such as overheating, two actions take place. One is an immediate correction of the problem; the other is the alerting of the crew by a warning light or sound. A crew member can then make a personal check to see if there is some undesirable situation that might cause other problems.

The computer programs that tend to the thousands of avionics functions and variations are all stored on tapes as mass memories. These functions are grouped in three basic subsystems:

(1) Guidance, Navigation, and Control

This relates to the manual or automatic control of the shuttle in all flight phases. Since the space shuttle is a combination of a launch vehicle, a space orbiter, and an atmospheric glider, its control varies greatly from one environment to another. Changes must be reacted to in split seconds, taking into account dozens—perhaps hundreds—of variables that relate to temperature, altitude, speed, light, external pressure, weight, payload, and other factors. The commander of the shuttle can elect to remain on automatic control and navigation, where the computer system flies the vehicle; control stick steering, where the crew does the flying with the help of the computer; and direct control, where there is no computerized assistance.

A number of different navigational aids are used, both in orbit and in atmospheric flight, to provide the computers and the crew members with information about the craft's position at any given instant. The star tracker is a good example, an instrument that constantly computes the location of the shuttle in relation to certain stars selected for this purpose. This is a sophisticated improvement on the age-old system used by mariners who navigated by setting the sights of their sextants on the North Star and other heavenly bodies while crossing vast stretches of ocean. Navigational aids on board the shuttle can instantly compute such data as altitude and speed, or measure the distance and approach to some other vehicle or object in space.

(2) Displays and Controls

The orbiter displays and controls subsystem allows the crew to supervise, monitor, and control all of the systems on board. The flight deck contains the most complicated assortment of displays and controls ever assembled in an aircraft. Although it might seem impossible for a pilot to keep track of the more than two thousand displays and controls, the process is simplified in a number of ways. One is the grouping of these units according to related functions. Another is the use of different types to indicate parallel information. There are, for example, different kinds of switches—toggle, push, horizontal, and rotary. Meters are designed in shapes that are symbolic of the kinds of information being shown—round, square, oblong, etc.

(3) Communications and Data Systems

The shuttle uses four separate communications systems, including microwave and ultrahigh frequency. These provide for the transmission and reception of voice, engineering and scientific data, and commands; television to the earth; closed-circuit television; internal communication; communication to other components in orbit; and tape recording. Supporting systems on the ground complete the communications network.

Astronaut Daniel Brandenstein (left) communicating with ground control.

A miniature television camera lens in this space suit helmet (above) will view what the astronaut sees during a space walk.

Some of the shuttle's onboard data processing hardware (below), also known as "black boxes."

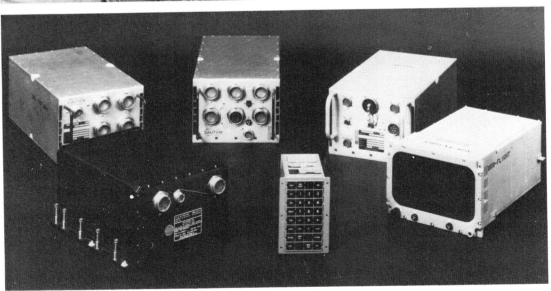

Astronauts floating in the shuttle cargo bay

The computer data programs needed to support the different avionics functions—the "black boxes"—are stored in tape mass memories. They are then transferred to the individual computer memories as called for.

In this manner, through the intricate network of avionics, all the systems on each space shuttle are linked together, and can be brought into operation instantly and harmoniously.

MID FUSELAGE

The mid fuselage is the largest single section of each shuttle. It is 60 feet long, 18 feet wide, and 14 feet high, yet relatively light, weighing only 14,000 pounds. In the mid fuselage is the huge cargo bay that carries equipment into space and brings back other units to earth.

The cargo bay has two rounded doors at the top that can be operated from the flight deck or from the bay itself. The payload bay is not

Astronaut Bruce McCandless II outside the shuttle near the robot arm

pressurized, so these doors can be opened or closed during flight at any time without affecting atmospheric conditions inside. They do, however, contain radiator panels (four on each door) that control the temperature inside the cargo bay to protect all or part of any payload during flight.

One of the most interesting devices on the shuttles is called the Remote Manipulator System (RMS). This is a fifty-foot-long robot arm that can be controlled easily from the flight deck. The crew can observe its operation through the aft windows on the flight deck or over the internal television system. The arm has joints that function like an elbow, wrist, and hand. It can lift objects from the cargo bay and place them in orbit. Or it can reach out into space and grasp a satellite as a shuttle is maneuvered alongside. Because of weightlessness in space, the arm has no trouble maneuvering extremely large and heavy objects.

Near the outer end of the robot arm is a small television camera with spotlights, so that the crew operator on the flight deck can see what the robot is doing. Each piece of cargo in the bay is clearly marked with identification symbols so that the operator can easily unload items in proper order. Additional floodlights are along each side of the payload bay, since many maneuvers are undertaken in darkness.

AFT FUSELAGE

The aft section is made up of two units: a short part of the shuttle's body, about eighteen feet long, joined to the ship's Orbital Maneuvering System and the wing controls; and the shuttle's main engines. The short fuselage section bears the load of the wings, the high tail fin, and the engines. At its rear, underneath the main engines, is the body flap. This is a flat, winglike section used during re-entry into the earth's atmosphere. It provides extra control, known as trimming, for the shuttle. In addition, it shields the main engines from intense heat.

THE WING

The right and left parts of the wing form the shuttle's *delta* shape, derived from the fourth letter of the Greek alphabet, which looks like a capital "A" or Δ when you observe the ship from directly above. The wing is about sixty feet long where it joins the fuselage, and as much as five feet thick. It has a honeycomb construction inside, and all parts are made of aluminum. Inside the lower wing surface is the main landing gear.

Vital features of the wing are the elevons. Elevons enable the crew to control the shuttle when it is operating as a glider in the earth's atmosphere—that is, after re-entry. The elevons function both as elevators, moving the ship up and down, and as ailerons, rolling it from side to side.

VERTICAL STABILIZER

The vertical stabilizer is the tail fin, which rises high above the rear end of the shuttle. It stabilizes the space shuttle and keeps it from rolling from side to side during atmospheric flight. The tail fin also contains the rudder. The pilot uses the rudder to turn the craft to the right or left. The pilot only uses it when the shuttle has returned to the earth's atmosphere.

Like the wing, the vertical stabilizer is made of aluminum with honeycombed skin panels. The rear panels on the rudder can be split in half, flaring out on each side to catch the air and serve as brakes when the shuttle is landing. This action also helps to stabilize the craft, an important feature since shuttles land at about 215 miles per hour.

THE PROPULSION SYSTEM

Three engines in the tail provide the main propulsion for the space shuttle. They use a mixture of liquid hydrogen and liquid oxygen for fuel, and are ignited on the ground just before each launch. After the solid rocket boosters separate from the shuttle and parachute to the ground, the three main engines continue to run. They consume a great deal of fuel. However, they remain in operation for only about nine minutes, by which time the shuttle is well on its way into orbit and requires no further power assistance.

The energy released by the three engines at full power level is said to be equivalent to the output of twenty-three Hoover dams! The high-pressure fuel pump delivers as much horsepower during this phase of the flight as twenty-eight diesel locomotives.

An interesting—and almost contradictory—fact about liquid hydrogen fuel is that it is the second coldest liquid ever made and is stored at −423 degrees Fahrenheit. Yet when it is combined with liquid oxygen, the temperature in the combustion chamber reaches 6,000 degrees Fahrenheit, higher than the boiling point of iron.

The engines are designed with another unique feature. They are mounted so that they can be swiveled or pivoted slightly to aid in steering or maneuvering the craft. Thus they control the exact angle of flight, a combination of movements known as pitch, yaw, and roll. In this way, the shuttle can be kept in the best possible trajectory to reach the desired point in space and move easily into orbit.

ORBITAL MANEUVERING SYSTEM

In addition to the three main engines, each space shuttle also contains a separate propulsion system known as the Orbital Maneuvering System (OMS). Its function is to thrust the shuttle into its selected orbit after it leaves the earth's atmosphere. It can later provide the thrust to move the ship from one orbit to another or to rendezvous with another spacecraft or satellite. It controls the speed of the shuttle in orbit, as well as the attitude (pitch, yaw, or roll) of the craft. Its final job, at the end of each mission, is to thrust the shuttle back into the earth's atmosphere.

The two orbital maneuvering engines are in the rear of the fuselage. These engines are capable of undertaking as many as one hundred missions in their lifetime.

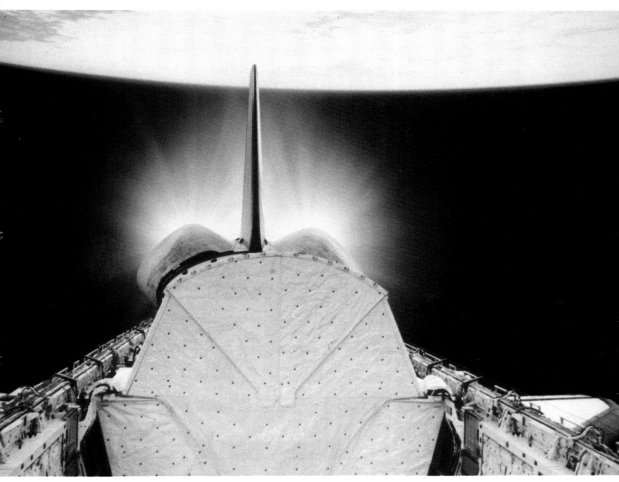

Test fire of *Columbia*'s Orbital Maneuvering System

OTHER CONTROL AND POWER SYSTEMS ON BOARD

Space shuttles contain equipment and facilities for living and working in space indefinite periods of time. Systems must not only be reliable and life sustaining, but must maintain the health and well-being of the crew and provide enough comfort so that they can function at a high level of efficiency. The following are a few of these vital systems:

Electrical Power. Four hydrogen-oxygen fuel cells supply all the electricity needed during the mission. These provide fourteen kilowatts of continuous energy, but can be boosted to twice that number for brief periods. Small turbines operate the pumps that provide hydraulic pressure. Pressure is needed, for example, to operate the landing gear, the rudder, and the elevons.

Environmental Control and Life Support. This system "scrubs" the cabin air so that it is always fresh and pure. It adds new oxygen as needed, keeps the air pressure the same as at sea level, heats and cools the air, maintains the correct humidity, and provides drinking and bathing water. Thus, the crew can work in a comfortable shirt-sleeve environment and all parts of the ship are protected from overheating, cold, or pollutants.

Pressurization System. Proper pressure inside the shuttle is vital, not only to keep the crew comfortable and healthy, but also to keep the structure of the craft stable. The forward part of the ship, including the flight deck and the crew's quarters in the mid deck, is designed with many small openings in the interior walls and floors so there is proper air flow to maintain even pressure throughout.

Air Revitalization System. Two cabin fans provide air circulation. The air is constantly channeled through a canister containing lithium hydroxide, which removes carbon dioxide, and charcoal, which neutralizes odors. The canister is changed regularly, just like the filters in an ordinary room purifier. The humidity is also carefully controlled.

Water and Waste Management. The water supply for the crew is a natural by-product of the fuel cells that generate electricity. This water is fed into storage tanks at a temperature of about 50 degrees Fahrenheit. When the water tanks are full, a relief valve automatically forces the excess water outside the spacecraft.

The waste collection system looks much like the toilet on an airliner, but collects both human wastes and kitchen garbage. As much as four pounds of water an hour is pumped down into the waste tank. (In space water does not flow, because there is no gravity. It simply hovers, as a blob, until forced into a container.)

Astronaut C. Gordon Fullerton preparing a meal. He holds a beverage in a squeeze dispenser. Packages of dehydrated foods are fastened to the locker doors with velcro.

The Kitchen. This is much like the small galley on a seagoing ship. The main difference is that each item of food and liquid is stored and locked down in such a way that it cannot float and become a nuisance or hazard. The galley area contains a food preparation center, food and equipment storage, hot and cold water dispensers, food trays, an oven, a water heater, and waste storage.

Fire Detection and Suppression. With so many highly flammable substances on board, each space shuttle has the most advanced kind of fire detection system. Each shuttle contains a minimum of four portable fire extinguishers and three fixed extinguishers. The hand extinguishers are designed with tapered nozzles so they can be inserted into "fire holes" on the electrical panels, to extinguish fires behind the panels. The extinguishers hold one of the most effective fire suppressants ever made. Instead of smothering the flame, it breaks its chemical chain reaction to put it out. A very small amount of the extinguisher's contents (less than 6 percent) is needed to suppress the average fire.

Taking measurements for heat-shielding tiles on *Columbia*'s upper wing surface

Nine early-warning smoke detectors sense smoke, as well as any significant increase in gases within the crew compartments or the areas where the sensitive avionics devices (''black boxes'') are stored. Should trouble arise, it is signaled by a warning light on the fire detection panel and by a siren.

Thermal Protection. One of the most vulnerable parts of any space shuttle is the outer skin at the moment when the craft is re-entering the earth's atmosphere and is subjected to extreme heat caused by air friction. This heat builds up only on those portions of a spacecraft that are heading into the atmosphere. In the case of the space shuttle, it is the underside and the nose. To counteract this intense heat build-up, the shuttle must be protected by some kind of layer that will absorb heat and dissipate it almost instantly. The first shuttles were referred to as ''flying brickyards,'' because they were covered for this purpose with thousands of silica glass tiles that were bonded to the belly, the underside of the wing, and the nose.

This thermal protection system has to do more than prevent the ship from burning up during the descent. It must also limit the temperature of the shuttle's aluminum structures to temperatures of 350 degrees Fahrenheit or less to prevent any external damage or internal weakening. Only then is the shuttle truly reusable, able to make round trips into orbit on a regular basis with minimum maintenance and repair.

The insulation on the underside of the shuttle consists of approximately twenty thousand tiles. These vary in thickness from half an inch to three-and-a-half inches, depending on the intensity of the heat at different locations. Other parts of the spacecraft are protected by thinner, lighter tiles, or by different types of insulation.

These are some of the major components that make the space shuttle one of the most versatile and remarkable transportation vehicles ever devised for any purpose, in the earth's atmosphere or beyond.

View of the shuttle returning to earth

Packages of experimental materials rest in the shuttle's payload bay (above). The northeast coast of Africa appears in the background.

PAYLOADS AND COMMERCIAL OBJECTIVES

4

At 11:05 in the morning of March 30, 1982, astronauts Jack R. Lousma, the commander, and C. Gordon Fullerton, the pilot, landed the space shuttle *Columbia* on an air strip in New Mexico. This was *Columbia*'s third orbital test flight, and by far the longest. It lasted more than eight days, orbited the earth 129 times, and covered almost *four million* miles. The flight's importance lay not in the distance covered, however, but in the fact that this was, as NASA reported, "the busiest and most demanding of the space shuttle missions . . . a major stride towards an operational spacecraft."

Astronauts Lousma and Fullerton

The two-man crew started and restarted the orbital maneuvering engines to simulate docking procedures when coming alongside other craft or picking up or discharging cargo. The huge mechanical arm was used repeatedly to develop the crew's expertise in grasping an experimental package. They used it to move an eight-hundred-pound package from its stowed position to other locations inside and outside the cargo bay. They retrieved the package from space several times and stowed it

Robot arm grasps a diagnostics package for an Office of Space Sciences experiment.

away again. They did all this simply by manipulating a hand controller that jutted from the control console. Reacting to the gentle pulse of human energy, transferred through electronic circuits, the long metal arm rose out of its cradle in the cargo bay and followed instructions, as any well-mannered robot should.

The robot transmitted each of its movements through miniature television cameras mounted on the arm. Even when the camera on the "wrist" was blacked out by a short circuit, the one on the "elbow" provided sufficient visual guidance.

Robot arm and cargo bay components, viewed against the Mediterranean Sea (on the right) and the Dead Sea (center).

Lousma and Fullerton fired the jet thrusters during one of the maneuvers, purposely causing *Columbia* to roll and pitch while they used the manipulator arm. But even these disturbances failed to cause any vibrations or loss of grip. In another type of test, they turned the shuttle so the cargo bay was exposed to the sun for twenty-eight hours, then away from the sun so they could check the operation of the curved doors during wide temperature variations. The only problem reported was some difficulty with the latches after the doors had been subjected to intense cold. This quickly resolved itself when the shuttle was rotated to allow the sun's rays to strike the top of the cargo bay and heat its surfaces.

"GETAWAY SPECIALS"

One of the long-range objectives of the space shuttle program is to offer transportation for relatively low-cost scientific experiments in space. The program has popularly been called the "Getaway Special"—an opportunity for industry, schools, professional organiza-

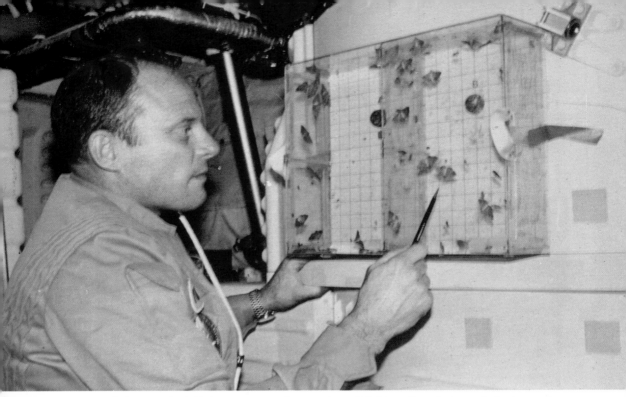

Astronaut Jack R. Lousma examines an insect flight motion study, a student experiment submitted by Minnesota high school senior Todd E. Nelson.

tions, and even individuals to conduct experiments in orbit. The getaways go on a space-available basis, in much the same way that some airline passengers are placed on a standby basis to wait for empty seats. The initial charges for transportation were relatively modest, from $3,000 to $10,000 for each payload container, and several hundred applicants were quickly enlisted to participate in future payloads.

NASA does not try to evaluate the scientific merit of any of these specials. But it does impose several rules. For one thing, the experiments must be serious and scientific. "We have no intention," says a NASA official, "of carrying merchandise into space simply so a marketer can sell items as souvenirs of a spaceflight." Also, the objective must be peaceful in nature, intended for the human good. And there can be no ingredients or components in any getaway canister that could explode or cause a fire.

To prepare for this program and to see what problems might arise, a payload canister was carried aloft and checked out under actual operating conditions. On later trips, some of the successful getaway experiments included testing fruit and vegetable seeds to see how they would function if planted on future space stations to grow food for the occupants; measuring the effects of the space environment on photographic film; and checking the reliability of computer memory circuits while in orbit.

One test explored the possibility of using weightlessness to produce microscopic particles that are more uniform in size and shape, and hence more effective. Experimenters were able to produce tiny latex spheres, suspended in a solution. These spheres are used to measure pores in the intestines and to conduct a certain type of eye research. If properly improved upon, these spheres might also be used to convey drugs for the treatment of cancer.

THE SPACE RACE GOES COMMERCIAL

A space-projects analyst for a major West Coast bank predicted that large corporations, both American and foreign, "will be to space what the Hudson's Bay Company was to North America: a source of exploration and financial enterprise. It's free enterprise carried to the twenty-first century."

It is a well-known fact that certain processes, besides the manufacture of chemicals and drugs, can be best achieved outside the pull of earth's gravity. Examples of these are the making of optical crystals, certain complex metal alloys, and glass of a very high purity. This type of glass might, in fact, be particularly useful in space. It could improve space telescopes and other instruments that would go into orbit or spin off in the farthest reaches of space to beam back information to the earth.

Surprising though it may seem, small processing plants could be put into orbit, completely unmanned, to manufacture certain types of products. They would only need to be attended to periodically, when

Astronaut Guion Bluford (above) exercises on a treadmill in an onboard medical test. Astronaut Jack Lousma (below) with equipment for separating cells according to their surface electrical charge. This is a forerunner to experiments that will purify biological materials in the low-gravity space environment.

the finished products would be removed and new batches of ingredients added.

One of the advantages of the shuttles over other types of spacecraft is that they can carry larger cargoes than unmanned rockets and manned capsules could carry. Even so, it quickly became apparent that it would be a long time before enough shuttles could be built to accommodate all of the organizations that wanted to make use of them. By the end of this century, there could well be a "merchant fleet" of shuttles making round trips into space, much like the huge fleets of oceangoing vessels that carried on international commerce at the end of the last century.

One group of investors has already offered to pay NASA for a commercial shuttle to be used exclusively by private business and industry. It would cost more than one billion dollars just to build the craft, plus the cost of sending it into orbit and bringing it back again. But such a shuttle would be capable of making about one hundred round trips before it had to be taken out of service or completely rebuilt.

Would it be worth $10 million per mission, plus the cost of launching and maintenance? Some businessmen think it would, since the cargoes could be large and varied and of great value. Also, it is becoming increasingly important for large communications corporations to place satellites in orbit to improve their services and give them a strong competitive edge in their fields. They have found, to their dismay, that cargo space on the shuttles has been booked into the late 1980s. Some have had to turn to foreign countries to locate space on rockets planned for the future.

NASA invites aerospace companies to send technical observers to the Kennedy Space Center and other facilities to see at first hand the steps involved in planning space missions and readying shuttles for launching and orbit. In the future launchings and other operations might be turned over to private contractors, who would work under NASA's supervision. Some shuttles would then operate as jets do, under one or more private companies.

FACTORIES IN SPACE

By the time NASA celebrated its twenty-fifth anniversary in October, 1983, the idea of building factories in space was no longer just a dream in a science fiction novel. It had already been proven that space shuttles could carry large loads of construction materials into orbit, where small processing plants could be built, with living quarters for small teams of technicians. NASA already had developed some mobile work stations that astronauts could use, by the 1990s, for construction operations in space. These work stations were designed so they could be constructed on earth, then folded up and shipped into orbit in the cargo bay of a shuttle. Once at their destination in space, they could be unfolded. Or they could be transported in modular units, much like prefabricated buildings, and reassembled in space.

Once the work station was in orbit, the crew could start to work. A team of working astronauts would strap their feet onto moving platforms that could travel either vertically or horizontally along a frame. The frame would also serve as a kind of conveyor belt, moving the prefabricated factory out into space and away from the shuttle as fast as it was assembled.

Why use a work station at all—isn't it just more equipment to be hauled into space? The answer is that work stations can be used again and again, and that they make construction work in space much easier. Without such work stations, the astronauts involved would float about freely in space. They would constantly have to use time and energy to reposition themselves around the structure being assembled. Without effective work stations, construction projects would be so time-consuming and the astronauts would become so exhausted that these projects would not really be practical.

Once assembled, the factories could begin functioning as soon as they were supplied with the necessary components and technicians. Most of the plants planned thus far are for making small amounts of substances or products that require a high degree of quality and purity. Drug products are good examples. So are optical products, such as a

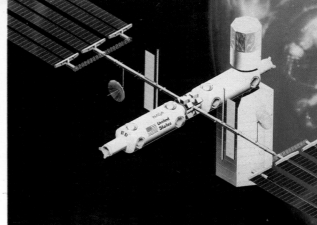

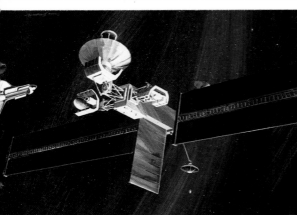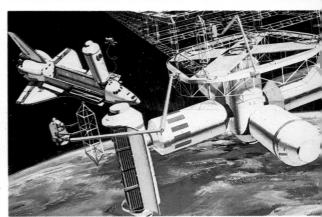

Artists' concepts of future space stations. The stations may include several modules for living quarters and experiments (top left), a hangar for other space vehicles (top right), or pallets to hold experimental payloads (bottom left). The space shuttle could transport new modules to be attached to the space station (bottom right).

type of glass that is totally flawless. Its use? Probably for some of the critical instruments to be used in space in the future.

The plans for a space station have already been laid out. They call for a structure two hundred feet long and one hundred feet wide. It would resemble a collection of shiny cans, flanked by large arrays of flat solar cells, which would collect energy from the sun and supply the power. This complex would contain laboratories, storage modules, and living quarters for half a dozen astronauts and technicians. Surrounding the space station would be unmanned platforms— "space factories"—for processing materials and manufacturing products.

Here are some examples of companies that are interested in using the shuttles and the space station for long-range projects:

St. Regis Paper Company. A space station would be used to observe the size and condition of trees in the company's thousands of square miles of forestlands. Remote sensing and recording instruments and equipment on board space stations can provide more accurate and detailed data than any present earth-based methods.

Boeing Company. Its Aerospace Division would construct a biochemical laboratory in space for perfecting new kinds of pharmaceutical products. It would also test new equipment and produce small quantities of biological materials for use in research. These products and materials would be purer and more effective than any now being manufactured on earth.

Battelle Columbus Laboratories. The company would like to conduct experiments to examine the growth of collagen, a fibrous protein that is the major component of connective tissue in humans and vertebrate animals. (Collagen is a major ingredient in gelatin and certain kinds of adhesives.) By working in an atmosphere with no gravity, researchers could control the shape and nature of these fibers and produce better materials for medical and health products.

Westech Systems. This company manufactures silicon crystals used as semiconductors in electrical and electronic equipment. By forming silicon in space, technicians can eliminate some of the defects in the crystals.

Many companies that have proposed such plans for space have been very specific about their requirements. Boeing, for instance, estimated that it would need about 170 shuttle flights to complete the initial stages of its project. Westech said that one phase of its plans could be completed during just four flights, but each flight must be three months long.

NASA is already working with commercial companies to plan joint research and manufacturing projects. One firm is engaged in research to determine how to manufacture biological proteins, such as hormones. It was discovered that a plant in space could produce seven

Astronaut Dale Gardner, in the manned maneuvering unit (MMU), docking with a spinning Westar VI satellite to stabilize it for capture and return to earth.

hundred times as much of a certain kind of protein as a similar plant on earth could produce using the same amount of ingredients. The company plans to complete a full-scale processing plant in space by the end of the 1980s. Such an operation would cost a huge amount of money at the start, but could be very profitable within a few years.

Any products manufactured commercially in space—at least until the end of the twentieth century—will have to be sold *at a very high price*. It costs more than $5,000 per pound to place materials and equipment in space, and about the same amount to bring the finished products back to earth. That is why manufacturing in space appeals only to companies that market very expensive products and materials. Some of the advanced semiconductor materials, for example, sell for as much as $50,000 per pound. One such material is called gallium-arsenide, a near-perfect formation of crystals that may one day replace silicon as the material for computer chips. Pharmaceuticals are natural candidates, too, because certain types are worth more than $1 million per pound.

ADVANTAGES TO WORKING IN SPACE

It is not always easy to understand the reasoning and economics behind commercial ventures in space. The answer lies in the conditions that exist in space, particularly the lack of gravity and the presence of a nearly perfect vacuum. On earth, the pull of gravity separates various components and prevents them from mixing evenly and consistently.

Take the case of the gallium-arsenide crystals mentioned on page 69. These crystals are grown from two basic ingredients: gallium (a bluish-white metallic element that is brittle at low temperatures but melts at just above room temperature) and arsenic (which, besides being poisonous, is metallic and crystalline in formation).

Since the gallium and arsenic have different densities, they tend to form crystals that are not uniform and pure. As one NASA scientist explained the problem: "It is like trying to make Jell-O with fruit in it. Gravity pulls the fruit to the bottom of the bowl before the Jell-O has solidified and you don't end up with a uniform mixture. In space, however, without that gravity, you'd end up with the fruit evenly spaced from top to bottom."

That is exactly what happens when forming crystals, drugs, or almost any other kind of mixture where it is important to have a uniform blending of ingredients.

Another advantage to processing materials in space is that they can be blended without having to hold them in containers. Molten metal, for example, forms a kind of spherical blob and requires only a tiny magnetic or electric field to hold it in one place. This is a great advantage when working with certain very expensive metals that become easily contaminated if placed in pots or holders made of other metals.

A good example is iridium, a silvery-white metal like platinum that melts at 4,400 degrees Fahrenheit. Iridium is very temperamental, and becomes brittle and hard to work with if it touches other metals while being treated. In space, it can be processed as a blob, without ever touching a container. The resulting iridium is much purer than that produced on earth and can be worth twice as much per ounce.

As the shuttle program has expanded, more and more nations besides the United States have shown great interest in participating and, in fact, have already become involved. Germany, Canada, and Japan, for instance, would like to lease American shuttles and facilities and eventually develop their own.

It is evident that NASA, and any private companies that go into joint ventures with it, will have a tough job keeping up with the growing demand. NASA has predicted that it will build its program to about three dozen shuttle launchings by the beginning of the 1990s. But that schedule seems hardly enough to satisfy the many companies that are eager to conduct commercial ventures in space.

Astronauts Dale Gardner (left) and Joseph Allen (on the mobile foot restraint) work together to bring Westar VI into the shuttle's cargo bay. Astronaut Anna Fisher controls the robot arm from *Discovery*'s cabin.

Charred interior of the *Apollo I* spacecraft, seen through the entry hatch. Three astronauts were burned to death in the tragic fire on Jan. 27, 1967.

Melted plastic from the protective shroud coats *Apollo I*'s nose cone.

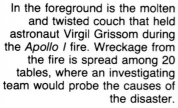

In the foreground is the molten and twisted couch that held astronaut Virgil Grissom during the *Apollo I* fire. Wreckage from the fire is spread among 20 tables, where an investigating team would probe the causes of the disaster.

MISSION OPERATIONS AND CONTROL

5

(WHAT HAPPENS WHEN THINGS GO WRONG)

"Shuttle Rises to Orbit, but a Fuel Cell Fails: Trip May Be Cut Short."

"Rocket Inquiry Delays Shuttle."

"Toxic Propellants Loosen Tiles, Threaten Lift-off."

These are but a few of the headlines that have appeared in newspapers, alerting us to the fact that the dramatic successes of America's space shuttles have also been tempered with frustrations, delays, a great deal of risk to the missions, and dangers to the astronauts involved.

In the past, the United States has fortunately had few catastrophic accidents involving death or injury to astronauts. But Americans, and particularly those who were at the launch site at the time, will never forget the flash fire aboard spacecraft *Apollo I* on the ground at Cape Kennedy, Florida, on January 27, 1967. Before they could be rescued from the flaming capsule, astronauts Virgil I. Grissom, Edward H. White, and Roger B. Chaffee were burned to death.

NASA officials, aware of several accidents that required crews to be ejected or take other emergency measures, are understandably cautious. Standard operating procedures call for delays, aborts, or early returns from orbit if systems fail and there is imminent risk to equipment or crew.

To the layman, a fuel spill sounds like a rather simple problem, one that happens occasionally to the family car, with no dire results. You simply mop it up if it's in the garage, flush it with water if it's on the engine, or perhaps just let the spilled gasoline evaporate and dry out. But on a space shuttle, a fuel spill can be deadly. One such accident occurred early one September morning when the space shuttle *Columbia* was being readied for a mission. A substance called liquid nitrogen tetroxide was being pumped into a tank near the nose of the shuttle. The mixture is used to fire the set of fourteen small jet thrusters that turn and rotate the shuttle in orbit.

Suddenly, almost immediately after the pumping operations began, a valve in the feed line malfunctioned. Although the spill was detected within seconds and only a few gallons had spilled, serious damage had been done. Nitrogen tetroxide turns into highly toxic nitric acid when exposed to moisture, as it was in this case. For that reason, workers cleaning up the spill had to wear special clothing and use a vacuuming device wherever the liquid had touched the shuttle's exterior surfaces. This acid acted so quickly that more than two hundred of the heat-resistant tiles that cover the shuttle had to be removed, cleaned, and replaced. The acid had loosened the cement that bonds them to the aluminum skin of the craft.

There was no alternative but to delay the mission.

In the case of the fuel cell that failed, the threat was obviously more serious because the shuttle was already in orbit. The touchy question facing NASA officials at Mission Control Center in Houston was whether to continue the mission, which had been scheduled to last five days in orbit, or to cut it short and scrap some of the valuable experiments planned many months in advance. The failure was all the more frustrating because the fuel cell was a standard item that had been used on just about every manned space flight made by Americans during the previous six years. It was as reliable and familiar to the astronauts as a good automobile battery is to a motorist.

The fuel cell was one of three on board, all designed to produce electricity for lighting, equipment, and other energy requirements.

Mission Control Center during the Fourth of July (1982) landing of the fourth shuttle mission.

Two fuel cells could do the job, perhaps with a slight cutback in the use of equipment. But in this case the problem was magnified because hydrogen was building up inside the cell. That meant possible danger, including explosion. The problem was solved eventually by cutting off the flow of oxygen and hydrogen to the fuel cell. But it was still up to Mission Control to decide whether to halt the mission.

Oftentimes, it is only when problems like this arise that the public is aware of the very tight linkage and communication that exist between a shuttle in orbit and the mission operations and support systems on the ground. The Mission Control Center is the heart of the system, once the launch has been successfully completed and the shuttle is in orbit. It is composed of the flight control room, a computer complex, and a number of staff support positions located around the main control room.

A Planning and Operations Management Team handles all the shuttle's preflight operations. This team plans, develops, and schedules all space flights. It coordinates the crew's training and inflight activities, manages communications, designs the flight, and sees that all preflight activities happen on schedule. This team also works with the Payload Operations Control Center, which is in charge of planning for the satellites, laboratories, and other cargoes, or "payloads," that will be transported into orbit.

75

MISSION CONTROL CENTER: FLIGHT CONTROL FUNCTIONS

Within Mission Control Center, the Flight Control Team is a vital unit. Located in the flight control room, this team directs shuttle operations from the countdown through the launch, the entry into space, the orbit, the re-entry into the earth's atmosphere, and the landing. The members of this team receive their assignments about nine weeks before a launch, and they live with the preparations day in and day out.

The basic Flight Control Team has special expert members on hand during the shuttle's launch, re-entry, and landing phases to assist in those operations. Once the shuttle is in orbit and traveling smoothly, the launch experts fade from the picture and the basic orbit team continues to direct the flight. The orbit team consists of four officers: the flight director, the communications engineer, the flight activities officer, and the payload officer.

These teams coordinate their activities with many other teams in many other locations. They are in touch with personnel at the launch sites, the main landing airfield, alternate landing fields, the Department of Defense, the Federal Aviation Agency, the United States

State Department, the Coast Guard, and the Network Operations Control Center, which is the focal point for space tracking and data compilation.

TRACKING AND COMMUNICATIONS NETWORK

The Tracking and Communications Network is made up of tracking stations that are scattered around the world. Each station puts the shuttle crews in contact with Mission Control, though for only several minutes at a time. Each is in contact with the shuttle during that brief time period when it passes directly over its zone of surveillance. Thus, Mission Control Center can be in almost continual contact with the shuttle on all of its orbits around the earth.

The original network consisted of thirteen stations on four continents: North America, South America, Australia, and Europe. Locations were on Ascension Islands; Santiago, Chile; Bermuda; Goldstone, California; Guam; Kauai, Hawaii; Madrid, Spain; Merritt Island, Florida; Orroral, Australia; Quito, Ecuador; Fairbanks, Alaska; Rosman, North Carolina; and Winkfield, England.

Special-purpose mobile stations were also located in strategic positions in Florida, Maine, and California. Supporting the network was a fleet of specially equipped planes known as Advanced Range Instrumentation Aircraft (ARIA). Under the jurisidiction of the U.S. Air Force, these flew to outlying parts of the world where ground stations were unable to support the shuttle missions.

Space tracking stations are equipped with a variety of antennas, each designed for a particular task. Functioning like giant electronic magnifying glasses, the larger antennas pick up signals transmitted from the spacecraft in a radio form called telemetry. Thus, if something goes wrong with any component of the craft or with its situation in space, the stations on the ground are instantly alerted.

In the event there is any kind of problem, the flight controllers can confer by voice with more than two hundred people in tracking and monitoring stations around the world. This makes it possible to study

Launch of the Tracking and Data Relay Satellite from space shuttle *Challenger*

all aspects of the problem and evaluate it quickly and effectively. Problem solving is assisted by a worldwide system of almost 150 computers located at the tracking stations. Pertinent information is funnelled from them to the main computers at the Mission Control Center, where it is instantly available to the flight controllers.

Improvements in this tracking system led to the development of a new system called the Tracking and Data Relay Satellite System. As the name suggests, it uses satellites to complement the ground tracking system. These new tracking stations in the sky have many advantages over the ground stations—one, of course, being that each is right on site, where the action is taking place. The tracking satellites are themselves carried into space by the shuttles, enclosed in the cargo bay, and then lifted out by the shuttle's robot arm and placed in orbit.

These space trackers transmit their data to ground stations that can process the information in split seconds and relay it to the flight controllers. Satellite trackers, which are built for a useful life of about ten years, possess tremendous transmitting capabilities. They can process as many as 300 million "bits" of information per second. Since it takes about eight "bits" to form one word, this is equivalent to processing three hundred sets of a fourteen-volume encyclopedia in a single second!

MISSION ABORTS

Whenever problems occur that are so serious that the mission must be aborted, flight controllers have three alternatives. The first is known by the code letters RTLS, which mean "Return to Launch Site." This emergency procedure is used if one of the main engines fails shortly after lift-off, but before the shuttle has gone into orbit.

After the RTLS command is given the crew of the shuttle continues moving skyward until the two solid rocket boosters have completed their normal thrusting operation and are separated and begin floating to earth on parachutes. The space shuttle, still with its external fuel tank attached, continues to thrust downrange, firing its two remaining main engines, its Orbital Maneuvering System, and its rear jet thrusters. It continues in this manner, using up fuel until there is just enough left to reverse the direction of flight and return to the landing strip at the launch site.

The crew then performs a "pitch-around" maneuver. This turns the shuttle around in the opposite direction, taking a little more than half a minute to swing around 180 degrees. The maneuver places the shuttle (still with its external fuel tank) in a "heads-up" position, pointing back toward the launch site. The command to cut off power in the main engines is given as soon as the shuttle has reached the correct altitude and heading, has settled into the proper speed, and is in a direct flight path angle to the landing site. The next command is to release the external tank. Since the shuttle's path has been over the ocean, the tank falls harmlessly into the water.

The pilot and crew then bring the disabled shuttle into a landing, gliding without power, but using jet thrusters if necessary to keep the ship under control. Since the landing will take place a relatively short time after lift-off, the chances are that air and ground and weather conditions will still be as favorable as at the moment of launching.

The second abort alternative is known by the code letters AOA, "Abort Once Around." This emergency strategy is used if a main engine fails shortly *after* the two solid rocket boosters have expended their fuel and been jettisoned by parachute, but before the craft has gone into orbit. By this time, the shuttle has flown so far downrange that it is a long distance from the landing strip at the launch site, and well out over the ocean. The safest procedure is usually to make one low orbit around the earth before preparing to touch down.

The crew keeps the two remaining main engines firing, but does not yet use the Orbital Maneuvering System or the rear jet thrusters. The main engines provide enough propulsion to reach what is known as an "intermediate orbit," one that is relatively low, or close to the earth. As the shuttle approaches this orbit, the main engines are cut off and the external fuel tank is jettisoned. The Orbital Maneuvering System is then fired, to maintain the low orbit for one complete circling of the earth. As the shuttle begins to approach the launch site, a second firing of the Orbital Maneuvering System moves the craft down into the earth's atmosphere again.

Now the shuttle is ready for the normal re-entry phase, the approach to the landing site, and a conventional touchdown.

The third abort alternative is the ATO, "Abort to Orbit." This procedure begins when one of the main engines cuts out unexpectedly as the shuttle is nearing orbit. After evaluating the situation, the controllers may decide that the shuttle should continue on its planned mission into space before making a final decision.

The crew continues firing the two remaining main engines for the normal time period, then cuts them off, jettisons the external tank, and proceeds into orbit. The orbital maneuvering thrusters are fired as planned, to insert the shuttle into its designed orbit. A decision is then made as to how many orbits the spacecraft will make and how long it will remain on its mission before re-entering the earth's atmosphere. If the failure of one main engine has been the only problem and all other systems are functioning properly, there is a good chance that the mission will continue as originally planned.

Picture of the space shuttle orbiter (top left), taken from a satellite orbiting above it

Astronaut Bruce McCandless (above) flying through space

Experimenting with the robot arm (left)

Opposite page: Space shuttle test vehicle *Enterprise* during rollout activities. "Chase planes" appear in the background.

"We're kind of busy up here.
What can we do for you?"

THE ASTRONAUTS

6

"We're kind of busy up here. What can we do for you?"

One of the early shuttle missions had a long list of experiments to be conducted by the two-man crew during a period of less than a week in space. As the experiments proceeded, however, so did a rash of minor problems that caused certain discomforts and added to the personal pressures and stresses on the astronauts. One of the two voice transmitters went dead, making communication difficult. A video camera on the robot arm failed, making it necessary to use binoculars when testing unloading procedures in the cargo bay; the toilet in the crew compartment broke down. The pilot was beset by motion sickness. The air freshener proved inadequate to the job. And one of the radios had a habit of giving off loud and unexpected static just as one or the other of the crew members was trying to get some sleep.

Perhaps it was a breach of space etiquette, but it was quite understandable when Mission Control asked the pilot a question about an experiment's progress and received the tart reply, "We're kind of busy . . ."

This particular mission, more than any other, convinced mission planners that they might be overworking shuttle crews with too many projects and not enough rest and relaxation. Astronauts had performed so well in NASA's many space programs over the years, often under great stress and in the face of unforeseen dangers, that they were thought of as super beings rather than ordinary humans.

Since then, more attention has been paid to relieving some of these stresses and to making sure the shuttle crew get sufficient sleep. One source of stress, oddly enough, is the immense exhilaration that can come during the launch and the initial stages of the entry into orbit. "This ride is a real barn burner!" exclaimed one astronaut when the ship was only three minutes or so off the pad. "Man, what a feeling! What a view!" shouted another into his microphone as his shuttle started circling the earth.

The exhilaration is fine, and certainly spontaneous. But there can follow a severe letdown once a routine is established and the crew is faced with its many tasks and responsibilities. This reaction is only normal. At such times, heartbeat is likely to increase markedly and blood pressure rise, especially in astronauts who are on their first ventures into space. Even the older hands, who take it more in stride, are likely to experience some emotional extremes. Thus, space psychology has become a vital factor in the selection, training, and scheduling of shuttle crews.

ASTRONAUT SELECTION AND TRAINING

"Spacemen of fiction—Jules Verne's travelers to the Moon, or the comic strip heroes Flash Gordon and Buck Rogers—were familiar characters midway through the twentieth century," said a fact sheet from NASA a few years ago, "but nobody could describe accurately a real astronaut. There were none."

It was not until 1959, the year after NASA was founded, that the space agency asked the United States military services to list candidates who met certain qualifications. The search was finally under way for pilots for the exciting new manned space flight program.

NASA was looking for pilots who had both jet aircraft flight experience and engineering training. It wanted graduates of test pilot schools who had a minimum of fifteen hundred hours of flying time. It further specified that the candidates had to be in top physical

Astronaut candidates in survival training. Left to right: Margaret Seddon, Kathryn Sullivan (the first woman to walk in space), Anna Fisher, Sally Ride (first woman to be a shuttle crewmember), Shannon Lucid (behind Ride), and Judith Resnik.

condition, under forty years of age, and (because of the space limitations of the Mercury capsule then being designed) slender and less than five feet, eleven inches in height.

More than five hundred pilots qualified, but the number was considerably whittled down after psychological and technical examinations were conducted, and after some of the candidates voluntarily withdrew. In the end, after even more stringent physical and psychological tests, seven pilots were selected as the first astronauts, from the navy, air force, and marines.

Three years after that first selection, NASA issued another call for candidates, reviewed more than two hundred applications, and pared the list to nine. By the time of the third recruitment, in October, 1963, the emphasis had shifted away from flight experience to superior academic records. The new breed of spacemen were called "scientist-astronauts" because all who met the minimum requirements held doctorates, or the equivalent experience, in the natural sciences, medicine, or engineering.

This academic emphasis has continued ever since, along with the requirement that candidates be in top condition, both physically and mentally. NASA conducts flight training once a selection is made

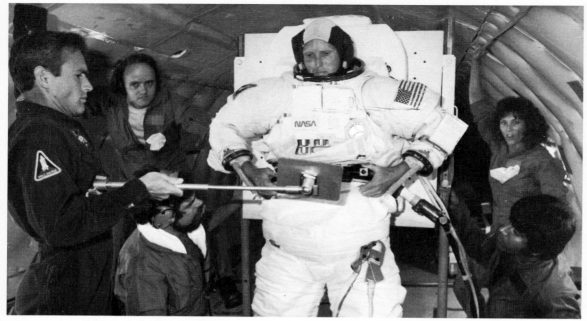

Astronaut C. Gordon Fullerton takes part in a suiting-up exercise, while specialist-astronaut William Fisher holds a mirror. This special suit is used during space walks.

from the ranks of the applicants. After that it's "back to school" for everyone in the program, regardless of previous educational experience or capabilities. Basic courses are science, technology, mathematics, meteorology, navigation, astronomy, physics, and computer operation and programming.

Astronauts-to-be are familiarized with weightlessness in the space environment through several methods that simulate this unique experience. In one such maneuver, they are flown in a jet "over the top" of a parabolic flight path, which gives the same effect as being in a rapidly descending elevator. During thirty seconds or so of zero gravity, the trainees practice common actions, such as eating, drinking, and manipulating small pieces of equipment. Longer periods of weightlessness are simulated under conditions of neutral buoyancy in a water tank holding full-scale models of the interiors of spacecraft.

In order to become accustomed to moving and working and living in pressurized space suits, astronauts spend a great deal of training time in these bulky outfits.

Much of the aircraft training is devoted to landing methods and procedures, especially gliding in at high speeds and with no power. Aircraft with characteristics similar to those of the shuttle are flown by the astronaut trainees from altitudes of 35,000 feet or more to dead-stick landings—that is, with no engine power. The fact is driven home hard, and often, in these sessions that there is no second chance, no possibility of climbing back into the sky and going around again in a space shuttle.

"You have *one* chance, and one only," emphasizes the instructor, "wherever you land, on the runway or a stand of cactus—*that's it!*"

Other astronaut responsibilities are discussed and reviewed. They include such matters as keeping abreast of all spacecraft developments; learning about the design and function of launch vehicles and facilities; knowing what kinds of payloads might be carried into orbit and what functions they will serve in space; and becoming thoroughly familiar with all types of ground facilities and personnel.

Because the space programs are so complex, no single astronaut can be expected to know about all the important changes that take

Left: Joe Garino, physical training specialist, designs an individual gym workout program for each crew member. *Right:* Astronauts training underwater for the weightless environment of space.

place in his program, often on a day-to-day basis. Thus, the trainees are assigned specific areas of the program. Periodically, they brief the rest of their group on new developments.

By the time astronauts are assigned to definite flight crews, their schedules have really become crammed. Crews are formed well in advance of launch dates, with several crews in training at any given time. During all this, they are expected to maintain peak physical condition and to keep their flying skills sharp.

Crew members all receive cross-training so they can handle the most demanding and critical duties of their associates in an emergency, or as replacements for any reason. In addition, during the early operational test flights, a second, or back-up, crew goes through the identical training. In this way, crew members who become ill or suffer some injury can be replaced before a flight with no delay and without in any way compromising the mission.

The tempo increases even more when the astronauts begin working with the various simulators—the mock-ups of flight decks and cargo bays and controls that are exactly like those on the actual flight. The simulators are realistic to the tiniest detail. Instruments are programmed to give the same readings about navigation or velocity or guidance that they would in flight. Hidden movie projectors show views of the earth, stars, the payload cargo bay, the launch pad, and the landing runway on the spacecraft windows as the shuttle ''moves'' from one situation to another.

''During earlier programs,'' says NASA, ''these simulated conditions were so accurate that most astronauts come back from a mission feeling they had made the same flight many times before.''

Training reaches its peak several weeks before the scheduled flight when the mission simulator is linked with the Mission Control Center. The tracking stations are also tied in, though in simulated form. The shuttle crews (both primary and backup) and flight controllers practice the entire mission in joint training exercises that are all but the real thing. This is the last major chance to iron out the bugs and make certain that the coordination is finely attuned.

Astronauts Anna Fisher (above) and Vance Brand (below) training in the space shuttle simulator.

Astronaut Sally Ride practices parachuting techniques during survival training.

By this time, the astronauts have learned to adapt themselves to long hours in cramped quarters. They also have checked out all of the equipment many times over, and have begun to feel comfortable in space suits of all kinds, including the ejection escape suit.

For many years, males dominated the field as astronauts, except in Russia, where the first female was sent into orbit as early as 1963. But all that changed in 1983 when an American flight crew included a woman. She was Dr. Sally K. Ride, a thirty-two-year-old physicist. Within a year, NASA had eight female astronauts in its ranks and was recruiting others.

That same flight included another "first," when a medical doctor was assigned to the mission. His job was to conduct tests to determine the causes of space adaptation syndrome, the fancy name for space sickness (a form of motion sickness) that plagued several astronauts during earlier flights.

During the mission, the doctor, Norman Thagard, performed tests on himself and other crew members, measuring the motion of fluids inside the body, increase in pressure inside the head, eye movement, and visual perception. Researchers believe that one cause of space sickness may be that the inner ear, which has some control over balance, becomes confused by the astronauts' weightlessness and by the fact that they are often in an upside-down position.

THE CREW

The shuttle crew regularly consists of the commander and the pilot. Additional crew members are a mission specialist who, like Dr. Thagard, makes the flight to monitor certain technical or scientific conditions, or to conduct experiments; and one or more payload specialists.

The commander and pilot operate and manage the shuttle during all phases of flight, from the launch to the final touchdown. Even when the flight is completed, their job is not done. They spend several hours, or even days, in debriefing. Using the log (diary) of the flight, they recount their experiences for the benefit of the controllers and

Dr. Norman Thagard (left), mission specialist, performing experiments to evaluate his physiological reactions in space. The "hop and drop" test (right) is used to study changes in the inner ear.

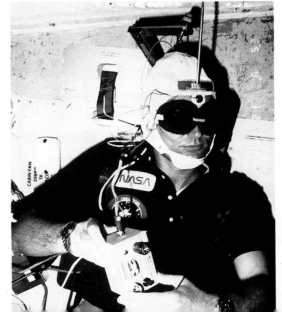

future crews. During the debriefing, they review all of the activities that took place to determine if the operating systems and procedures, the handling of cargo, or even the training before the flight might be improved.

The commander is responsible for the safety of the crew and protection of the spacecraft. He has the authority during the flight to change the flight plan or operational procedures if necessary. The pilot, second in command, would take over if the commander were incapacitated for any reason and could not handle his duties properly.

The mission specialist carries out predetermined scientific assignments. These could include conducting experiments or monitoring the performance of certain types of equipment. In some cases, this specialist would also work with the payload equipment carried in the cargo bay. During launch and recovery, the mission specialist might be assigned to monitoring and controlling the payload.

The payload specialists manage and conduct experiments relating to payloads used for research purposes. If the payloads are being placed in orbit for active, operational purposes (as in the case of communications satellites, for example), the payload specialists follow instructions from the agencies or organizations that have contracted for placing the payloads into orbit. But the specialists also have to coordinate all activities and procedures with the commander and pilot, since the safety and effectiveness of the ship and crew take priority over individual payload missions.

Payload specialists must complete rigorous courses of training, in addition to the basic training required of all astronauts. If they are joining the shuttle crew simply to perform assignments on board or next to the ship during the removal of equipment from the cargo bay, they go to school for some 180 hours, over a period of about four weeks. If, however, they also will be involved with a module in space alongside which the shuttle will dock, their training time is extended. Training time is extended, too, in cases where the payloads are unusually complex or require special skills and knowledge for their handling and operation.

The four *Spacelab* payload specialists walk through experiment procedures in the *Spacelab 1* mockup. Left to right are: Drs. Byron Lichtenberg and Michael Lampton (U.S.), Wubbo Ockles (the Netherlands), and Ulf Merbold (West Germany).

CREW ACCOMMODATIONS, EQUIPMENT, AND SCHEDULES

All crew members follow daily routines. These routines vary a great deal according to the number of astronauts on board, the length of the mission, and the nature of the assignments. Time must be allotted to each person for rest, work, meals, personal hygiene, and relaxation. Generally, each day is divided into an eight-hour sleep period and sixteen-hour waking period, rotating the schedule so at least one person is always on duty.

There are three one-hour meal periods, scheduled as close to normal mealtimes as possible. The galley and dining areas are in the mid deck and are composed of a food preparation center, storage area, hot and cold water dispensers, a pantry, a water heater, an oven, and waste disposal equipment. Uniquely designed food trays minimize the frustrations of trying to dine in an environment where everything is weightless and where, indeed, a person might be eating upside down.

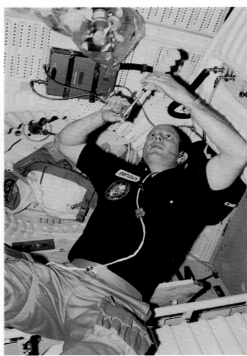

Astronaut John Young and specialist Ulf Merbold (left) prepare food in the mid-deck. Astronaut Jack Lousma (right) injects water to prepare a juice drink.

EATING ABOARD THE SHUTTLE PRESENTS SPECIAL PROBLEMS.

Astronaut Thomas Mattingly (left) opens a drink container with scissors. A selection of menu items (right) is strapped into a locker.

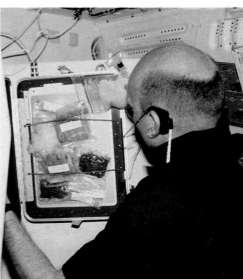

There are no food freezers or refrigerators on board the shuttle. The shuttle's food consists of individual servings, packaged in cans, semirigid plastic containers, and pouches. Some are in their natural state, while others are dehydrated, irradiated, or otherwise preserved. Because there is always plenty of water on board, a by-product of the fuel cell functions, dehydrated foods are very practical to store and recondition. Here are some typical space shuttle menu selections:

Breakfast: Peaches, scrambled eggs, bran flakes, cocoa, orange drink, beef patty, coffee

Applesauce, sausage, cornflakes, breakfast roll, granola with blueberries, grape juice

Lunch: Corned beef, asparagus, bread, pears, peanuts, lemonade, cold tea

Frankfurters, turkey tetrazzini, rolls, almond crunch bar, bananas, apple drink

Dinner: Shrimp cocktail, beef steak, rice pilaf, broccoli au gratin, fruit cocktail, butterscotch pudding, tropical punch

Cream of mushroom soup, smoked turkey, mixed Italian vegetables, vanilla pudding, strawberries, cookies, coffee, tea

Crew members rotate in performing various housekeeping tasks that may take from ten to fifteen minutes at given intervals during the day and night. Typical chores are cleaning waste compartments, dumping excess water, washing the dishes (usually with sanitized "wet wipes"), and putting the garbage out.

The sleeping accommodations are unusual—they can be either horizontal or vertical. Some look like sleeping bags. Others, more rigid, are referred to as "sleep stations." But they contain some components not found on most beds, such as the "sleep restraint." This holds the sleeper in position so that he or she does not float into the middle of the cabin. Another difference is that there are no

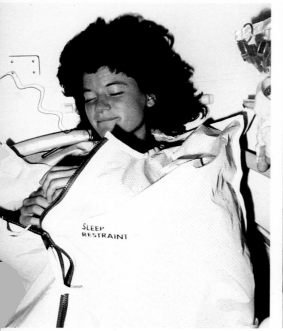
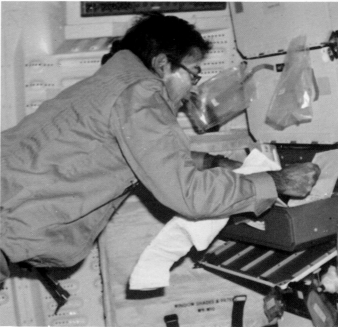

Left: Astronaut Sally Ride in her sleep station.
Right: Astronaut John Young cleaning his razor after shaving.

mattresses or pillows, which are hardly needed since the sleeper's body does not press downward and require comfortable support.

Other useful accessories are ear plugs and eye masks to block out the noises and lights that continue relentlessly while the shuttle is in flight.

The personal hygiene system is very important to all members of the crew. This includes the toilet and waste facilities, a station for brushing teeth and washing, and special kits that can be used in the weightless atmosphere for ordinary tasks such as hair care, shaving, or care of the nails.

The lack of gravity in the personal hygiene station presents special problems. When water is used for washing the hands and face, it has to be squeezed manually through a valve. Washcloths are moist and saturated with cleaning solutions. The waste collection system collects liquid and solid wastes, processes them to kill bacteria and eliminate odors, and stores them in condensed and dehydrated form until after the shuttle has landed.

Another standard item of equipment aboard the shuttle is the medical system. This has provisions for treating minor illnesses and injuries, as well as for treating astronauts who are severely ill or injured and keeping them in stable condition until they can be brought back to earth. Kits in this system contain equipment to assist the crew in treating patients through consultation with flight surgeons in the Mission Control Center.

Medical kits in the shuttles are more complex and sophisticated than most household first-aid kits. The kits contain such items as bandages, medications, injectable drugs, surgical instruments, a stethoscope, catheters, a blood-pressure gauge, tourniquets, syringes, intravenous tubing, tongue depressors, disposable thermometers, sterile gloves, an ophthalmoscope, eye patches, and many other first-aid items.

All in all, the space shuttle crews are well equipped to take care of all their needs and emergencies, short of an outright disaster.

Astronaut C. Gordon Fullerton takes a nap. Some astronauts choose to sleep with their feet or upper bodies anchored, and others use the sleep restraint bag.

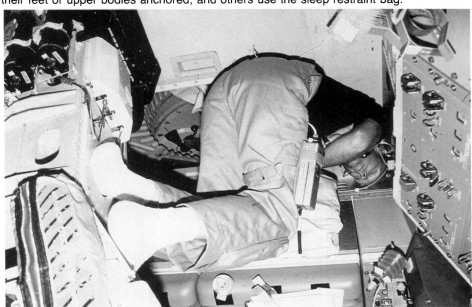

"We Deliver!"

SPECIAL MISSIONS AND RESEARCH
7

"We Deliver!"

That was the theme for the fifth shuttle mission, in November, 1982. In most respects, the mission was much like earlier ones, with the usual countdown, crew assignments, orbiting pattern, and eventual landing at an air force base in California. What made it stand out, however, was that it was the first operational mission—the first with a purpose beyond research and experimentation.

The space shuttle "opened for business" by transporting and deploying two communications satellites into orbit. The satellites were not NASA's, but were owned by two commercial companies, Satellite Business Systems and Telesat Canada. After about six hours of taking computations and positioning the shuttle, once it was in space, the clamshell doors of the ship opened and the robot arm lifted the two satellites and placed them outside the cargo bay. The release of powerful springs at just the right moment started the satellites spinning away from the shuttle at a rate of three feet per second.

"They're all yours!" said the shuttle commander, turning control of the satellites over to their owners, SBS and Telesat. The shuttle pilot then rotated the shuttle and changed orbit slightly to remain well clear of the spinning instruments.

The significance of this event is that a new space age had just begun. Shuttles would now be used to place instruments and modules and platforms in the sky for permanent operational use. Six months later, the new space shuttle *Challenger* improved on this feat by

Left: Launch of the Satellite Business Systems communications satellite

Left: The TDRSS satellite is gently mated to its Inertial Upper Stage, which will propel it to a higher orbit after it leaves the shuttle cargo bay. *Right:* The satellite is inspected inside the Vertical Processing Facility at Kennedy Space Center.

transporting a new type of communications platform into orbit and positioning it there. This was the first spacecraft in NASA's new Tracking and Data Relay Satellite System (TDRSS). It was to be used as a communications center to aid further missions of American space shuttles. These tracking satellites aid the ground tracking stations and one day may replace them entirely.

The TDRSS satellite was the heaviest object—about 5,000 pounds—ever to be carried aloft by a shuttle.

The way was now clear for shuttles to transport complete instruments into space, as well as building materials for a variety of construction projects in space: factories, solar power stations, communications centers, dwelling units, space telescopes, laboratories, and many other installations.

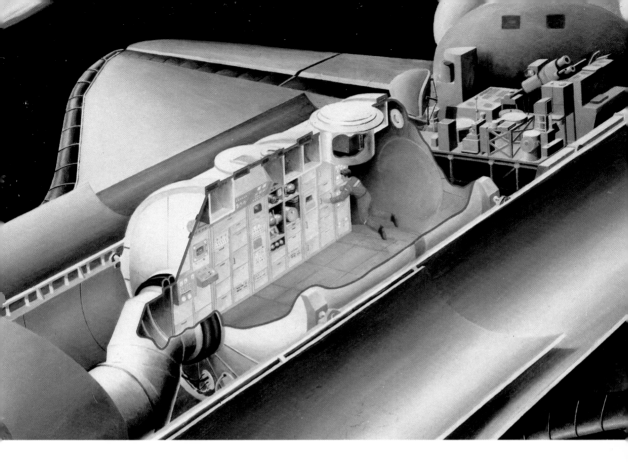

SPACELAB

The major forerunner of laboratories in space is the *Spacelab*. It is a manned laboratory first tested when it was carried into orbit in the payload bay of a shuttle in late November, 1983. There, while circling the earth, it served as a laboratory for more than seventy experiments over a ten-day period. By the end of the first week alone, scientists were predicting that the research being done in the lab would produce significant advances in atmospheric studies, astronomy, solar physics, biology, and materials processing.

Some scientists who had planned experiments for this mission had been waiting as long as seven years for *Spacelab* to become a reality. It was constructed to have a lifetime of five years and to be able to complete as many as fifty missions.

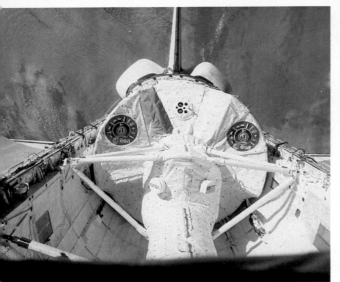

Left: The first onboard photo of the active *Spacelab* module in *Columbia*'s cargo bay. In the foreground is the docking tunnel leading to the shuttle's forward compartment. *Right:* Payload specialist Dr. Ulf Merbold inserts a scientific sample into a furnace for processing in the materials science rack.

    Spacelab was developed by the European Space Agency (ESA) for international research expeditions. It fits into the payload bay of the shuttle. The *Spacelab*'s two principal components are the pressurized module, with a laboratory where astronauts can work in shirt sleeves under normal earth-environment temperatures; and the open pallet deck, on which materials and equipment are exposed to space.

    The pressurized laboratory is connected to the flight deck of the shuttle by a tunnel. An air lock can also be attached to the lab, so that astronauts in space suits can go outside the ship to conduct tests or take observations. The pallets outside the pressurized lab are U-shaped and rather small—only ten feet in length. Basically, they are platforms for mounting instruments, but they can also heat or cool equipment, provide electrical power, and furnish electronic connections for feeding data from the experiments. The pallets are designed for instruments requiring direct exposure to space, or equipment requiring an unobstructed field of view. Such equipment might be radar units, sensors, antennas, and telescopes.

    The astronauts who are directly involved with *Spacelab* projects are called payload specialists. Although they may be nominated for the

102

flight by organizations that have paid for laboratory space, they are trained and certified for missions by NASA. As many as four payload specialists may be aboard during a *Spacelab* mission.

More than two thousand world scientists applied for participation in the first *Spacelab* missions in the 1980s. Ultimately NASA and the European Space Agency selected proposals from 222 scientific investigators from fifteen countries. Here are some typical *Spacelab* experiments:

Earth Surveys. These studies compile much data that can be useful in transportation, urban planning, environmental control, farming, fishing, navigation, weather forecasting, and prospecting.

Industrial Technology. The lack of gravity makes it possible to manufacture certain kinds of very expensive products and materials, such as chemicals and crystals, that are purer and more effective than those that can be made on earth. The manufacture of new types of alloys also has great promise.

Aerial photographs provide useful data for urban planners, meteorologists, environmentalists, and many others. At left is the San Francisco Bay area, taken from *Skylab*. Space shuttle *Columbia* photographed Eleuthera Island, Bahamas (right).

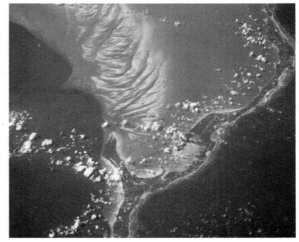

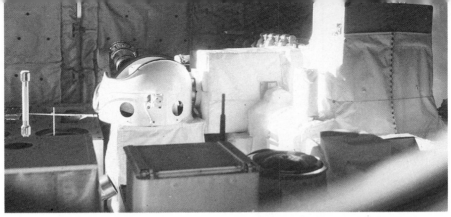
An array of *Spacelab* tests on the experiment pallet in the rear of *Columbia*'s cargo bay. The European Space Agency had twelve *Spacelab 1* projects; NASA had five.

Biomedicine. Zero gravity provides significant advantages in separating and purifying biological particles. Space processing provides greater opportunities for removing impurities from vaccines and for isolating cells or antibodies for the treatment of disease.

Astronomy Observations. In space, it is possible to make highly accurate studies of high-energy radiation such as gamma rays, X rays, and ultraviolet light. This radiation does not pass through the atmosphere in such a way that it can be accurately studied on earth. Locked into the findings are secrets about the origins, nature, and evolution of celestial phenomena.

Life Science. Studies of humans and other living forms in space show that zero gravity causes certain metabolic changes. Continuing research will help scientists understand these changes and will contribute to the advancement of medicine.

THE SPACE TELESCOPE

Human beings have always been intrigued by the stars and the moon and the heavens. Many cultures and religions have looked to celestial happenings to explain the past and present and foresee the future. Until the beginning of the seventeenth century, when Galileo and other early scientists invented the first practical telescopes, the heavens remained complete mysteries. By the nineteenth century, telescopes were amazing the world with discoveries of new planets and other celestial bodies.

Left: The Long Duration Exposure Facility (LDEF) carries materials being tested for possible use on a space station. Deployed in April, 1984, the LDEF is left in orbit for close to a year. The test materials are then analyzed for durability.

Below: Artist's concept of *Spacelab*

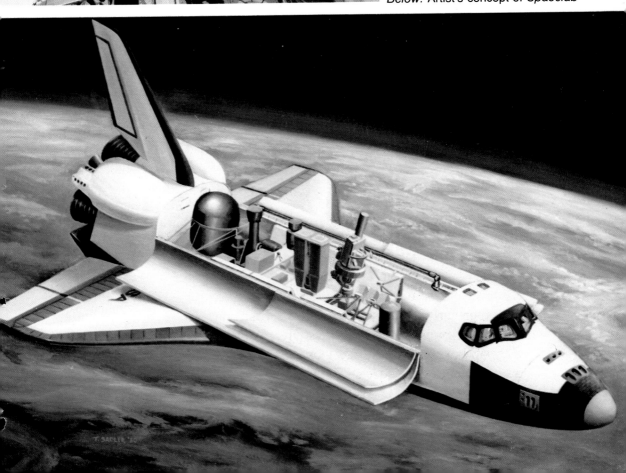

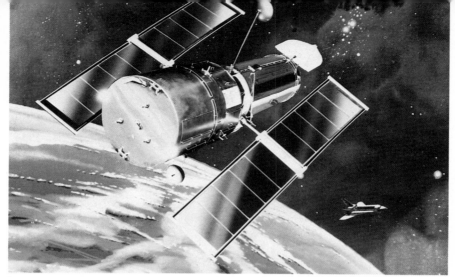
Solar panels supply the space telescope with energy from the sun.

But the most powerful telescope on earth could not begin to compare with a rather moderate-sized telescope positioned in space—even though it might be only three hundred miles or so closer to the heavens than one on top of a mountain peak in California.

Why should this be so?

The answer is that a space telescope is free of atmospheric interference, such as haze, pollution, filtering, and reflected light. These handicap even the most advanced earthbound instruments like the famous Hale telescope at Mount Palomar, California. Although the space telescope has a lens diameter of only 95 inches, as compared with Mount Palomar's 200 inches, it will be able to detect objects in space that are fifty times fainter. It will "see" objects seven times clearer than ground-based observations. In all, it will expand the visible universe by 350 times.

The space telescope consists of three parts: an optical telescope assembly; technical instruments such as a wide-field camera, a camera to photograph very faint objects; and spectrographs to examine the spectrum. An attached support systems module contains a very precise pointing and control system, a communications system, a thermal control system, and the power system. Electrical power is supplied by long solar panels, which use energy from the sun.

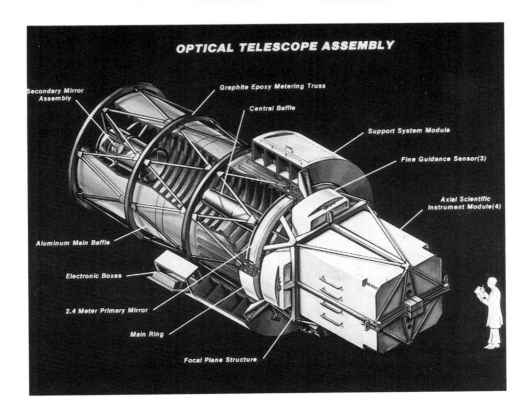

Secondary Mirror Assembly

Graphite Epoxy Metering Truss

Central Baffle

Support System Module

Fine Guidance Sensor(3)

Axial Scientific Instrument Module(4)

Aluminum Main Baffle

Electronic Boxes

2.4 Meter Primary Mirror

Main Ring

Focal Plane Structure

One of the major challenges is to focus the telescope on distant targets without wavering. NASA has described this as "equivalent to expecting a rifle marksman in Boston to zero his sights on a baseball in Los Angeles!" So it is easy to see why the pointing and control elements are crucial.

In operation, light enters the open end of the twelve-ton telescope, is projected by the primary mirror onto a smaller secondary mirror, and from there deflected to the scientific instruments for analysis. The telescope can make ultraviolet and infrared measurements not possible on earth. It will reveal many phenomena that cannot be seen—or can be seen only indistinctly—by telescopes on earth. Among these are enormous celestial dust clouds, gaseous nebulas, black holes, galaxies that are still being formed, exploding galaxies, and many rare varieties of stars.

Nearby, more familiar planets, stars, comets, and other bodies that lie within one hundred light years (one light year is about six million

The space telescope will enable scientists to gaze seven times farther into space than is possible now.

miles) will be subjected to very detailed scrutiny by the telescope. The study of plasmas (masses of gas) or mysterious quasars (objects that resemble stars) in space could unlock the secrets of new energy sources far beyond present expectations. Closer observation of the planets in the earth's own solar system will help explain the changes that are taking place in our world. For example, it might provide clues to ways we could better preserve our environment and avoid air and water pollution.

The tube-shaped space telescope, some 43 feet long and 14 feet wide, is designed and planned to function for at least fifteen years while in orbit. It can be serviced and repaired in space, using shuttles that can dock alongside it, hoist it on board, and provide technical maintenance. It could also be brought back to earth for major repairs or improvements. Since the telescope may have a tendency to drift to a slightly lower orbit (as happens with many objects in space) over a long period of time, space shuttles can easily be deployed to give it a lift back up into its proper orbit, 310 miles above the earth.

OTHER TYPES OF SPECIAL MISSIONS

There is almost no end to the kinds of equipment space shuttles can transport into orbit. Some of this equipment could be launched into much higher orbits, or even projected toward other celestial bodies. One example is the solar sail, being planned for an unmanned voyage to the moon. In operation, it resembles an enormous, silvery kite that is square in shape and slightly crisscrossed or corrugated over its entire surface. When carried aloft in a shuttle's payload bay, the solar sail looks like an oblong box connected by a thick rod to a cylindrical box of about the same size. The plan is to launch the sail with a booster rocket from the shuttle into a thousand-mile-high orbit, where it is free of any drag from the earth's atmosphere. There, a mechanism in the oblong base forces a set of spars to unroll. As they do so, they pull the lightweight material of the sail outward. A second set of spars finishes the job by extending the folds or pleats of the sail until the surface is completely open.

Now the sail is ready to move. But how?

Streams of photons from the sun—tiny particles of radiant energy—exert their force on the sail, much as the wind does on a ship's sail at sea. This steady force propels the sail in ever-widening orbits until it reaches the moon. The steering is automatically controlled by a movable mast and triangular vanes at the corners of the solar sail. It would take as long as two years before this unique space vehicle would finally swing leisurely around the moon.

As yet, the solar sail has no useful purposes other than testing out the concept itself. But if the moon voyage were successful, the sail could be a prototype for solar craft that could carry instruments—and some day perhaps even people—into the far reaches of space.

Another vehicle being developed—this one with specific objectives—is the space tug. As the name implies, these tugs would be used to haul other space vehicles and instruments, the same way seagoing tugs move ships and barges. They would be unmanned and remote controlled, and would remain permanently in orbit, not mak-

An artist's concept of the space tug

ing round trips to earth like the shuttles. Among their uses would be: to move payloads from the shuttles into higher orbits; to move satellites back into their proper orbits after they have lost altitude; to move modular units back and forth when construction projects are underway in space (such as the building of a space factory); or to gather satellites and instruments that are to be transported back to earth by a waiting shuttle.

Space tugs would be relatively small craft. Somewhat octagon-shaped, they might be no larger than about fifteen feet in diameter and three or four feet in length. Their useful life span would depend a great deal upon their power supply, largely solar energy. But an average space tug could remain in orbit for many months and perform dozens of useful jobs before being brought back to earth for maintenance.

These are but a few of the special-purpose vehicles that will enhance the usefulness of space shuttles and broaden their future scope of operations.

Astronauts Charles Conrad and Joseph Kerwin exit *Skylab 2* for extravehicular repairs.

Astronauts David Leetsma (left) and Kathryn Sullivan perform an in-space simulation of refueling another spacecraft in orbit. Sullivan was the first American woman to perform extravehicular activity in space.

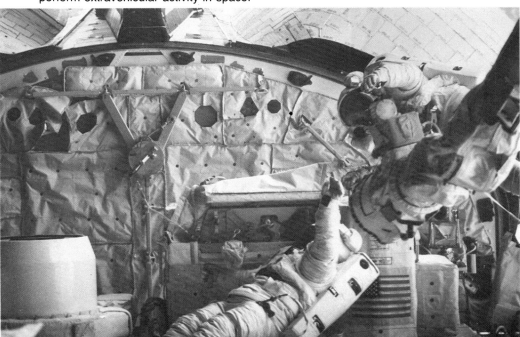

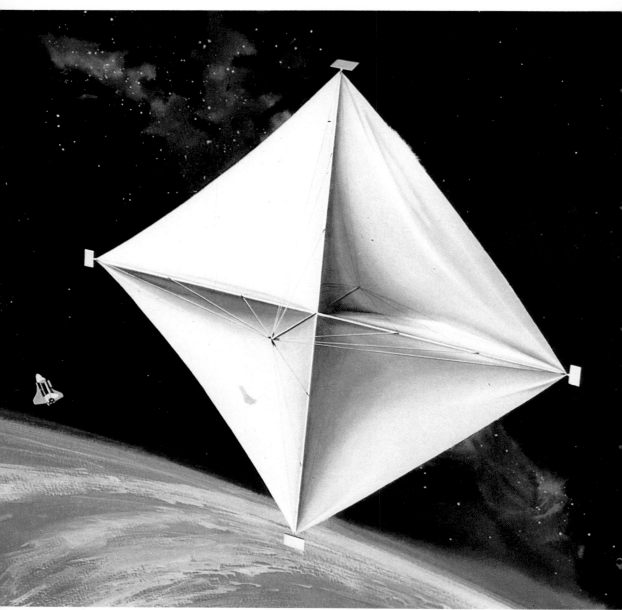

The solar sail is powered by photons from the sun.

THE FUTURE

8

The astronauts are shown in the drawing as they float weightlessly inside their space capsule, touching neither the floor nor the ceiling while being transported at great speed far beyond the earth's atmosphere. Only the quaint costumes they are wearing give away the fact that the adventuresome space voyage is being undertaken, not near the end of the twentieth century, but over a hundred years ago.

Weightlessness—fantasy and fact. *Left:* "The Effects of Weightlessness in the Space Projectile," from Jules Verne's *From the Earth to the Moon. Right:* Astronaut Robert Crippen in zero gravity aboard the *Columbia*.

The sketch was rendered for one of the most popular books of its day, Jules Verne's *From the Earth to the Moon*, published in 1865. Many of Verne's novels, and those of other authors who became famous for works of science fiction, were astonishingly accurate in showing what might happen to explorers who ventured into that great unknown world of outer space.

Can we be as accurate today in forecasting what will happen in space a century from now?

Scientists like to think so, as they feed huge amounts of data into computers and come up with calculations that are sheer wizardry at pinpointing the course of a spacecraft heading for the moon or a distant planet. For the near future, NASA planners and other space scientists see different types of space stations as a major objective, since these are within the realm of present technology. These space stations would be constructed, piece by piece, from parts carried into orbit by shuttles.

Space stations would start out as unmanned centers made up of a command and control module, heat-dissipating radiators, and solar arrays—wings that resemble the long blades on an old-fashioned ceiling fan. The whole structure would have an earth weight of slightly more than twenty thousand pounds. (It would, of course, be weightless in orbit.) Although its solar panels would extend some 185 feet each, they would be ingeniously folded for transportation in the payload bay of a shuttle.

This kind of smaller, less complex space station would be visited periodically by astronauts aboard a shuttle, who would check its condition, performance, and the instruments on board. This concept gives the space stations two operational capabilities that the shuttles do not have: long-duration operations in orbit and large amounts of electricity.

Later, the station would be increased in size and complexity to include research laboratories, living quarters, extra power facilities, a portable crane for assembling new spaceship components, a satellite repair shop, and other instruments and data-recording devices. This

The space station is likely to be evolutionary in character. It would start small and grow in size and capability over time. The first element would be the "utility section" (left), with power and communications systems for the station. Later, other elements, such as a pressurized module for astronauts (below), could be added.

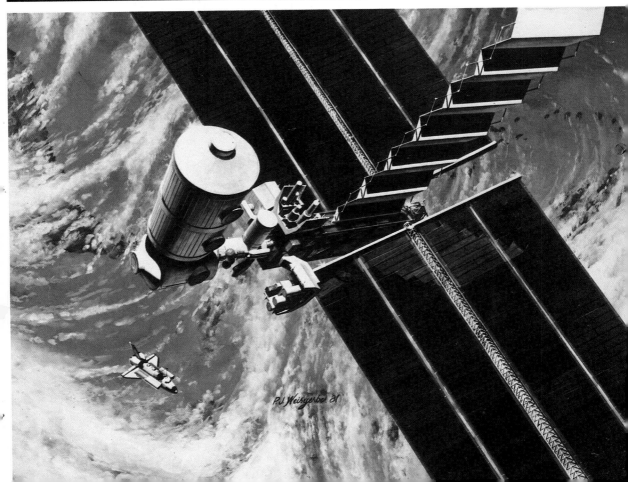

Syncom IV satellite leaves *Discovery*'s cargo bay in a "frisbee-like" deployment.

more sophisticated version of the space station would also serve as a way station for interplanetary travel and exploration. It would be located in an orbit about 250 miles above the earth.

The station would also be equipped with a high-energy orbital transfer vehicle, which could be used to boost other space vessels into a much higher orbit. Some of the unmanned satellites, for example, would be shot into orbits as distant as 22,300 miles from earth, an ideal position for communications satellites.

Most people working on a space station like this would live there for several months. Some astronauts and scientists, however, would be commuters, traveling back and forth by shuttle to perform specific short-term jobs. The stations, also referred to as space operations centers, would be equipped with small vehicles, the counterparts of mopeds on earth, to transport astronauts from one area to another.

Permanently orbiting space stations are considered to be "future events." Yet they have been in the active planning stage as far back as the early 1960s. Many scientists and engineers have felt they should be given higher priority. Great enthusiasm was generated, of course, when the Apollo spaceships began landing on the moon. NASA had

Syncom IV, moments after its release

hopes then that Congress would authorize a budget for space stations. But only the space shuttle itself received the necessary funds. The success of the shuttle flights then served to attract new interest in a space-station program that would be feasible for the 1990s.

THE SUPER-SHUTTLE

Another practical dream for the near future is a space shuttle that can carry larger payloads, remain longer in space, have greater supplies of energy, and roam into more distant orbits. Such a ship would have extra tanks of propellants for its maneuvering engines and jet thrusters, fuel cells with increased capacities, and some form of equipment to generate power using solar energy. This new breed of shuttle would probably have twice the carrying capacity of present shuttles, with much larger payload bays and more than one robot arm for moving the cargo.

With this super-shuttle in orbit, other space facilities could be joined with it to carry on operations that might last several months. The *Spacelab*, for example, could hook up with the shuttle for missions like continuous observations of the sun through two or more twenty-eight-day solar cycles, or the study of small plant or animal specimens through several generations in space. The shuttle would be on hand to carry in its payload bay all the components and supplies needed for that specific project but not intended to be left in orbit.

The super-shuttle might contain a small factory for constructing beams and other supporting structures in space, rather than having to transport them in prefabricated form from the earth. A so-called automated beam builder has been conceived by an aerospace company. It could form triangular girders from compact coils of ultralight metal. With the shuttle in position at the building site in space, the metal would be fed through rollers to shape it and form beams. As each beam was completed, it would be fitted to others making up the structure. The beams would be strong, yet so light (less than one hundredth the weight of comparable ones on earth) that a single shuttle flight could supply and fabricate enough material to build a space structure six hundred feet long, three hundred feet wide, and ninety feet high.

One of the major projects that might use this kind of construction is the solar power station. It would have a two-fold purpose: (1) to provide energy for nearby projects in space, and (2) to convert solar energy into power and then beam the power down for use on earth. The prospects of capturing solar energy in large quantities is particularly appealing because it would cut down on the use of hydrocarbons (oil, gas, coal, etc.) and thus eliminate a great deal of air and water pollution on earth. Solar power stations would be safer than present-day conventional power plants on earth because they would be far removed from populated areas, could easily dispose of excess heat without harming people or the atmosphere, and would greatly help to conserve our natural resources of metals because of their extremely lightweight construction.

The sun could be used to convert solar heat directly into electricity. Or it could be used to drive generators that produce electricity using any other form of energy. Space shuttles would be used not only in the initial construction of the solar power station, but in shuttling supplies and equipment on a regular basis, transporting personnel, and in some

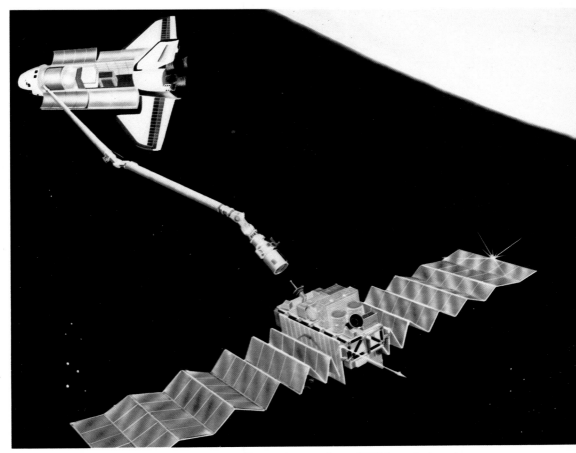

EURECA 1, planned by the European Space Agency for a 1987 launch, is a free-flying, retrievable space platform. Remaining in orbit for up to six months, the platform facilities will house metallurgical, biological, and biochemical experiments.

cases moving components from one position to another.

One of the more futuristic dreams involving fleets of space shuttles is to use them for transporting materials not only *to* the moon, but *from* it. Some scientists who have proposed the colonization of space by humans have also suggested that the moon be mined to exploit its many mineral resources. The ore would be refined on the moon, then transported to locations somewhere between the moon and the earth, where it would be fabricated into space structures. One of the big advantages of using the moon for this purpose is that, because of low gravity, it would be much easier and cheaper for space shuttles to be

launched from the moon with heavy loads. Landing, too, would be easier and safer because the pull of gravity is so much lower on the moon than on earth.

Other dreams about future space shuttles are less utilitarian. One NASA consultant is convinced that by the year 2000 there will be a hotel in space that can accommodate more than one hundred people. Package tours would allow a family to take a round-trip flight by shuttle, live in the hotel, spend a week in orbit, and take side trips to various space structures.

Look for it in the travel section of your daily newspaper in, say, the spring of 2001: ''Space Vacation for Four; All Expenses Included; Round Trip in the New Space Shuttle *Orbit Adventurer*, beginning July Fourth!''

Now that the space shuttle has joined the steamboat and the railroad train and the airplane as a major form of transportation, just about anything under the sun can happen.

Above: Discovery crew celebrates after successfully retrieving the Westar satellite from orbit. *Front,* David Walker, Anna Fisher, and Joseph Allen; *back,* Dale Gardner and Frederick Hauck.

Left: NASA's giant solar array experiment panel extends from *Discovery*'s cargo bay on its maiden flight. The structure, higher than a 10-story building, began as a folded stack only 3 inches thick.

SPACE ACCOMPLISHMENTS

SCIENCE & TECHNOLOGY

LAUNCH DATES	SPACECRAFT	EVENTS
April 12, 1961	Vostok I	Y. Gagarin of Russia makes the world's first manned flight, a single orbit, taking one hour and 40 minutes.
Feb. 20, 1962	Friendship 7	John Glenn becomes America's first astronaut, making three orbits in just under five hours.
Oct. 12, 1964	Voskhod I	Russia makes the first multiple-manned space flight, sending three cosmonauts in a single vehicle on a 15-orbit flight.
March to Dec., 1965	Gemini vehicles	The United States completes five flights, each carrying two astronauts. One sets a record of 206 orbits during almost 14 days.
March to Nov., 1966	Gemini vehicles	America completes five more flights, each carrying two astronauts.
Oct. 11, 1968	Apollo 7	America sends three astronauts on a 10½-day, 163-orbit mission, in preparation for a later moon trip.
Dec. 21, 1968	Apollo 8	American astronauts Borman, Anders, and Lovell complete the first lunar flight, taking six days and three hours and circling the moon.
May 18, 1969	Apollo 10	A second lunar flight, lasting eight days, is made by three American astronauts, Stafford, Cernan, and Young.
July 16, 1969	Apollo 11	The major goal of the *Apollo* program is achieved during an eight-day flight to the moon by astronauts Armstrong, Aldrin, and Collins. The first two make a lunar landing on July 20, while Collins orbits the moon in the command ship.
Nov. 14, 1969 to Dec. 7, 1972	Apollo vehicles	The United States completes five more lunar landings, sending three astronauts on each mission and accomplishing important research.

122

LAUNCH DATES	SPACECRAFT	EVENTS
May 25, 1973	Skylab 1 Skylab 2	Three American astronauts spend 28 days in space, orbiting the earth 405 days while completing laboratory experiments in space.
July 28, 1973	Skylab 1 Skylab 3	Three other American astronauts spend almost 60 days in space, orbiting the earth 859 times and conducting experiments.
Nov. 16, 1973	Skylab 1 Skylab 4	In the most ambitious Skylab program, three Americans remain in space for 84 days, conducting experiments during 1,214 revolutions of the earth.
July 15, 1975	Soyuz XIX Apollo	The first joint mission by the United States and Russia takes place when the *Apollo* docks with *Soyuz* and the two crews test equipment and techniques for possible future international rescues in outer space.
1977, 1978	Enterprise	The first space shuttle "orbiter," designed solely as a prototype, is put through a series of tests, including riding "piggyback" on a conventional jet plane to check its design.
April 12, 1981	Columbia	A new era in space flight begins as *Columbia*, piloted by John Young and Robert Crippen, orbits the earth for more than two days and makes a perfect landing. This is the first airplane-like landing of a craft from orbit.
Nov. 12, 1981	Columbia	The second flight of *Columbia* marks the first time that a previously used spacecraft has been successfully used for another mission.
March 22, 1982	Columbia	In a flight lasting more than eight days and covering almost four million miles, *Columbia* proves its ability to be used for important scientific missions.
June 27, 1982	Columbia	The seven-day flight achieves "near-flawless" completion of missions. Programs include medical research, measurements of the space environment, and tests to determine the shuttle's capacity for carrying various payloads.
Nov. 11, 1982	Columbia	The fifth space shuttle mission carries two commercial communications satellites and releases them in space. The crew is upped to four, double the number on previous flights, including two "mission specialists."
April 4, 1983	Challenger	A lighter, stronger space shuttle, with greater carrying capacity, makes its maiden voyage. It carries a crew of four and launches a large relay satellite towards a very distant point in outer space.

123

LAUNCH DATES	SPACECRAFT	EVENTS
June 19, 1983	Challenger	The flight, with a crew of five, includes Dr. Sally K. Ride, the first American woman to go into space. The six-day mission makes first test of launching, then retrieving, a satellite.
Aug. 31, 1983	Challenger	The crew of five on this eighth space shuttle mission includes the first U.S. black astronaut, Lt. Col. Guion S. Bluford, Jr. of the Air Force. A weather-communications satellite is successfully launched and used for calls to earth. *Challenger* makes first night-time landing.
Nov. 28, 1983	Columbia	On a nine-day mission, the improved *Columbia* carries a European-built research laboratory (*Spacelab*) into orbit and conducts scientific tests. The crew is increased to six.
Feb. 3, 1984	Challenger	Five astronauts ride the space shuttle into orbit and deploy two communications satellites, one of which becomes lost in outer space. Two crew members float free outside *Challenger* and test tiny ''jet thrusters'' on their backpacks for maneuvering themselves in space.
April 6, 1984	Challenger	The Long Duration Exposure Facility (LDEF) was put into orbit. The LDEF, with hundreds of experiments in trays mounted to its exterior, is scheduled to be retrieved and returned to earth in 1985.
Aug. 30, 1984	Discovery	After three postponements, the new shuttle *Discovery* is launched with a crew of six, including Judith A. Resnik, the second American woman to go into space. One project is the launching of three communications satellites.
Oct. 5, 1984	Challenger	Successful tests are made of the orbital refueling system for refueling other spacecraft while in orbit. Astronaut Kathryn D. Sullivan becomes the first American woman to perform extravehicular activities.
Nov. 8, 1984	Discovery	The malfunctioning Westar VI satellite is retrieved from space and stowed in the shuttle cargo bay for return to earth.
Jan. 24, 1985	Discovery	Shuttle crew launches top-secret spy satellite for the U.S. military.

GLOSSARY

SCIENCE & TECHNOLOGY

abort. To cut short or break off an action or operation of a shuttle or other mission because of equipment failure.

actuator. A mechanism that supplies and transmits energy for the operation of other mechanisms.

airlock. A hermetically sealed chamber used for passage between modules in a spacecraft that have different air pressures.

attitude. The position of a space vehicle, either in motion or at rest.

avionics. Contraction of ''aviation'' and ''electronics.'' Refers to the use of electronics in space flight.

barometric switch. Any switch operated by a change in atmospheric pressure.

blackout. The fadeout of radio and other broadcast transmissions during a flight because of the high speed of the spacecraft and atmospheric conditions.

bulkhead. A dividing wall used to withstand different pressures in a spacecraft, and also to provide access between compartments.

burn. The firing of a rocket engine.

burnout. The simultaneous burning of fuel and oxygen until the fuel is exhausted.

critical temperature. A temperature below which a gas may be transformed into a liquid by pressure.

cryogenic. Referring to extremely cold temperatures.

damping. Suppressing vibrations.

decoder. A device for translating electric signals into various functions that have been predetermined.

deorbit burn. Firing of a backward-acting rocket to slow down the velocity of a space vehicle.

dish. A parabolic (dish-shaped) reflector used as a radio or radar antenna.

docking. The act of joining two or more objects, such as spacecraft, in orbit.

drogue parachute. A small parachute used to pull open a larger parachute from a storage container or to slow down the descent of a spacecraft.

elevon. A horizontal control surface that combines the functions of an elevator and an aileron.

fairing. Part of a structure used to reduce air resistance.

footprint. The area in which a spacecraft is intended to land.

fuel cell. A device that converts chemical energy directly into electrical energy.

g. The symbol that represents the acceleration caused by gravity.

gantry crane. A large crane mounted on a platform that runs back and forth on parallel tracks near the launching platform.

heat exchanger. A device for transferring heat from one fluid to another without inter-mixing the fluids.

hot test. A test of a propulsion system conducted by actually firing the propellants (also called *hot firing*).

housekeeping. The term for routine tasks aboard a space vehicle to keep the craft in habitable and operational condition.

inclination. The angle between the plane of an orbit and a reference plane on earth, usually the equator.

launch azimuth. The initial compass heading of a space vehicle at the time of launching.

mockup. A full-sized replica of a space vehicle or other craft, used for testing and training.

multiplexing. The simultaneous transmission of more than one signal through a single broadcasting path.

nozzle. The portion of the rocket chamber in which the combustion gases are accelerated to a high velocity.

ordnance. Any devices that are pyrotechnic (flaming) in nature.

ordnance train. A network of small explosive charges, usually used to help maintain, or change, a craft's position.

pitchover. The turn that a rocket takes as it follows an arc and points in a direction other than vertical.

real time. The time during which the *reporting* of an event is done at the same time the event is taking place.

riser. A strap used to attach a parachute to an astronaut or a mechanical object.

rocket engine. An engine that contains both fuel and an oxidizer and can therefore be operated in the absence of air (as in outer space).

roll. The rotation or movement of a space vehicle around its longitudinal (lengthwise) axis.

rollout. The part of a space shuttle landing that takes place after it has touched down on the ground.

shirt-sleeve environment. The cabin environment in a space vehicle when it is similar to that on the earth's surface and does not require a space suit.

solenoid. A coil of one or more layers that contains an electrical current.

solid-state device. A device that uses the electric and magnetic properties of solid materials.

Spacelab. A portable scientific laboratory for performing experiments while in orbit.

station keeping. The sequence of maneuvers that maintains a space vehicle in its planned orbit.

telemetry. The science of measuring quantities, transmitting the results to a distant station, and evaluating and recording the data transmitted.

thermal conductivity. The capacity of a substance to conduct heat.

thrust. The pushing or pulling force of an aircraft or rocket engine.

thrust vector. The direction of the thrust force.

torsion. The state of being twisted.

transducer. A device that converts one form of energy into another (such as solar energy into electrical energy).

transponder. A combined receiver and transmitter whose function is to transmit signals automatically when triggered.

trim. Adjustment of a space vehicle's controls to achieve stability in flight.

truss. An assemblage of structural members (such as beams) that form a rigid framework.

ultrahigh frequency. A very high broadcasting frequency.

umbilical. A servicing line for fluids or electricity, attached from the ground to a space vehicle before its launching.

vernier engine. A small rocket engine used mainly to make fine adjustments in the direction and velocity of a vehicle in flight.

vertical stabilizer. A component of a space vehicle that consists of a fin and rudder assembly and helps to stabilize the craft's flight.

yaw. The rotation of a space vehicle about its vertical axis.

INDEX

SCIENCE & TECHNOLOGY

About The Authors

Wilbur Cross, a professional writer and editor, is the author of some 25 non-fiction books and several hundred magazine articles. His subjects range widely from travel and foreign culture to history, sociology, medicine, business, adventure, biography, humor, education, and politics. He has touched on these and other subjects in the course of profiling space shuttles.

Mr. Cross worked for several years as a copywriter and was an associate editor at Life magazine. Married and the father of four daughters, he lives in Westchester County, New York.

A 1972 graduate of Bronxville Senior School, Bronxville, New York, Susanna Cross attended Ohio Wesleyan University and studied at the School of Visual Arts in New York City.

Ms. Cross is president of FIRST FEATURES, Inc., a marketing and communications company she recently founded in Nashville, Tennessee. She is also an independent songwriter, and the co-author of NASHVILLE FEVER, a romance novel that was serialized in more than 100 newspapers through Universal Press Syndicate.